FIRST GRADE
1

ABA CURRICULUM FOR THE COMMON CORE

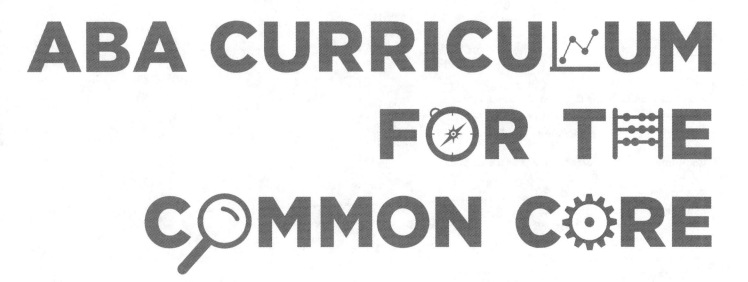

Programs and Materials for Teaching ELA and Math
in Special Education Using Applied Behavior Analysis

By Sam Blanco, MSEd, BCBA
for Different Roads to Learning

Different Roads
Tools for kids on the spectrum since 1995.

ABA Curriculum for the Common Core: First Grade
Programs and Materials for Teaching ELA and Math
in Special Education Using Applied Behavior Analysis

Copyright © 2015 Different Roads to Learning, Inc.

Published by
Different Roads to Learning, Inc.
121 West 27th Street, Suite 1003B
New York, NY 10001
tel: 212.604.9637 | fax: 212.206.9329
www.difflearn.com

Printed in the United States

Library of Congress Number: 2015945078
ISBN Number: 978-0-9907083-4-6

This book is dedicated to all the classroom professionals
who devote countless hours to the science of teaching.

— Sam Blanco

Table of Contents

FOREWORD 9

CCSS OVERVIEW 10

HOW TO USE THIS CURRICULUM

    Common Core State Standards and Special Education 25

    Applied Behavior Analysis 25

        Data Collection 26

        Preference Assessment 28

        Pairing 28

        Motivation and Reinforcement 29

        Discriminative Stimulus 31

        Prompting 31

        Generalization 33

        Natural Environment Teaching 33

    Considerations and Resources Related to Language Development 33

USER GUIDE

    How To Use This Kit 36

    Strand Reference Page 37

    Standard Reference Page 38

    The Big Picture 39

STANDARDS

    English Language Arts

        Reading: Literature 41

        Reading: Informational Text 53

        Reading: Foundational Skills 67

        Writing 91

        Speaking and Listening 101

        Language 115

    Mathematics

        Operations and Algebraic Thinking 157

        Number and Operations in Base Ten 175

        Measurement and Data 191

        Geometry 199

APPENDICES

    A. Preference Assessment 207

    B. Encouraging Social Interactions and Conversations 215

    C. Data Sheets and Samples 221

        Per Opportunity Individual Data Sheet 222

        Per Opportunity Group Data Sheet 224

        Per Opportunity Graph 226

        Task Analysis 228

REFERENCES 233

Foreword

We're thrilled to introduce this pioneering curriculum to teach each Common Core standard in special education settings. The Common Core is vague at best when it comes to its application to students with special needs, autism, and developmental disabilities. This curriculum aims to bridge the gap by equipping teachers with a companion curriculum that specifically addresses the learning needs of students in Special Education using the evidence-based principles of Applied Behavior Analysis. The kit provides both the materials and programs to teach each First Grade standard in English Language Arts and Math.

Our kit details each Common Core standard along with the Teaching Procedure, Discriminative Stimulus (Sd), and Materials required for teaching. The critical component of each program is the list of targets that drill down into the standard. It breaks each Common Core standard down into prerequisite skills that students need to master in order to meet the standard. Each task is presented within a data sheet so that the instructor may notate when the target was introduced, when it was mastered, and if it has been generalized for each student. Comprehensive Data Sheets for accurate record keeping are included, along with samples of how to complete them. In addition, a thorough how-to guide presents the main tenets of Applied Behavior Analysis (ABA), giving staff an accessible understanding of Motivation and Reinforcement, Pairing, Prompting, Generalization, Natural Environment Teaching, and Data Collection.

The key emphasis is on providing meaningful access to the standards by ensuring that we are teaching at a student's current skill level. By drilling down into each standard and breaking it into teachable steps and relying on the data collected for each student, we ensure that we are teaching at the edge of our students' abilities. Furthermore, by breaking each standard down and drilling into the prerequisite skills, the opportunity exists to use these First Grade programs for older students who are not developmentally able to meet grade-level standards.

The materials included in the kit have been carefully selected to not only assess and teach each standard and prerequisite skill, but to be wonderful additions to any classroom setting. The materials are versatile and can be used during more intensive teaching and one-to-one, as well as during center time and for independent play.

The goal of this curriculum kit is to make the Common Core accessible and relevant to students with autism and special needs. By equipping educators with teachable steps for each and every standard and pairing the teaching with motivating, versatile materials, the *ABA Curriculum for the Common Core* puts First Grade students in Special Education on the path to achieving success.

— Different Roads to Learning

English Language Arts

In the table below, you will find each Common Core State Standard (CCSS) listed by Strand, Cluster, and Code, along with the correlating Kit Materials. This grid serves as a quick reference of the CCSS and the items from the *ABA Curriculum for the Common Core Kit* that you'll need for teaching.

STRAND & CLUSTER	CCSS CODE	STANDARD	DRILL DOWN*	TEACHING MATERIALS**
STRAND: READING/LITERATURE				
Key Ideas and Details	RL.1.1	Ask and answer questions about key details in a text.	RL.K.1	• *Parts of a Story Thumball* • Classroom reading materials
	RL.1.2	Retell stories, including key details, and demonstrate understanding of their central message or lesson.	RL.K.2	• *Graphic Organizer Flip Chart* • *Tell the Tale Thumball* • *Retell a Story Cubes* • Classroom reading materials
	RL.1.3	Describe characters, settings, and major events in a story, using key details.	RL.K.3	• *SpinZone Magnetic Whiteboard Spinners* • *Write-on/Wipe-off Crayons* • *Retell a Story Cubes* • *Graphic Organizer Flip Chart* • Classroom reading materials
Craft and Structure	RL.1.4	Identify words and phrases in stories or poems that suggest feelings or appeal to the senses.	RL.K.4	• *Graphic Organizer Flip Chart* • Classroom reading materials
	RL.1.5	Explain major differences between books that tell stories and books that give information, drawing on a wide reading of a range of text types.	RL.K.5	• *Graphic Organizer Flip Chart* • Classroom reading materials
	RL.1.6	Identify who is telling the story at various points in a text.	RL.K.6	• *SpinZone Magnetic Whiteboard Spinners* • Classroom reading materials
Integration of Knowledge and Ideas	RL.1.7	Use illustrations and details in a story to describe its characters, setting, or events.	RL.K.7	• *Speaker's Box* • Classroom reading materials
	RL.1.8	(RL.1.8 not applicable to literature)	N/A	N/A
	RL.1.9	Compare and contrast the adventures and experiences of characters in stories.	RL.K.9	• *Graphic Organizer Flip Chart* • Classroom reading materials
Range of Reading and Level of Text Complexity	RL.1.10	With prompting and support, read prose and poetry of appropriate complexity for grade 1.	RL.K.10	• Classroom reading materials

*If your student has not met the prerequisite skills for this standard, drill down to the Kindergarten standard referenced here.

**Teaching Materials listed in italics are included in the kit; those not italicized are not included and can be found in your classroom.

English Language Arts

STRAND & CLUSTER	CCSS CODE	STANDARD	DRILL DOWN*	TEACHING MATERIALS**
STRAND: READING/INFORMATIONAL TEXT				
Key Ideas and Details	RI.1.1	Ask and answer questions about key details in a text.	RI.K.1	• *Graphic Organizer Flip Chart* • *Parts of a Story Thumball* • Classroom reading materials
	RI.1.2	Identify the main topic and retell key details of a text.	RI.K.2	• *Parts of a Story Thumball* • *Graphic Organizer Flip Chart* • Informational text
	RI.1.3	Describe the connection between two individuals, events, ideas, or pieces of information in a text.	RI.K.3	• *Graphic Organizer Flip Chart* • Classroom reading materials
Craft and Structure	RI.1.4	Ask and answer questions to help determine or clarify the meaning of words and phrases in a text.	RI.K.4	• *SpinZone Magnetic Whiteboard Spinners* • *Write-on/Wipe-off Crayons*
	RI.1.5	Know and use various text features (e.g., headings, tables of contents, glossaries, electronic menus, icons) to locate key facts or information in a text.	RI.K.5	• Classroom reading materials
	RI.1.6	Distinguish between information provided by pictures or other illustrations and information provided by the words in a text.	RI.K.6	• *Drawing Conclusions Reading Comprehension Cards*
Integration of Knowledge and Ideas	RI.1.7	Use the illustrations and details in a text to describe its key ideas.	RI.K.7	• *Drawing Conclusions Reading Comprehension Cards*
	RI.1.8	Identify the reasons an author gives to support points in a text.	RI.K.8	• *Graphic Organizer Flip Chart* • Classroom reading materials
	RI.1.9	Identify basic similarities in and differences between two texts on the same topic (e.g., in illustrations, descriptions, or procedures).	RI.K.9	• *Graphic Organizer Flip Chart* • Classroom reading materials
Range of Reading and Level of Text Complexity	RI.1.10	With prompting and support, read informational texts appropriately complex for grade 1.	RI.K.10	• Classroom reading materials

*If your student has not met the prerequisite skills for this standard, drill down to the Kindergarten standard referenced here.

**Teaching Materials listed in italics are included in the kit; those not italicized are not included and can be found in your classroom.

English Language Arts

STRAND & CLUSTER	CCSS CODE	STANDARD	DRILL DOWN*	TEACHING MATERIALS**
STRAND: READING/FOUNDATIONAL SKILLS				
Print Concepts	RF.1.1	Demonstrate understanding of the organization and basic features of print.	RF.K.1 (RF.K.1.a–1.d)	*See:* RF.1.1.a
	RF.1.1.a	Recognize the distinguishing features of a sentence (e.g., first word, capitalization, ending punctuation).	RF.K.1 (RF.K.1.a–1.d)	• *Sentence Building Dominoes*
Phonological Awareness	RF.1.2	Demonstrate understanding of spoken words, syllables, and sounds (phonemes).	RF.K.2 (RF.K.2.a–2.e)	*See:* RF.1.2.a, RF.1.2.b, RF.1.2.c, RF.1.2.d
	RF.1.2.a	Distinguish long from short vowel sounds in spoken single-syllable words.	RF.K.2 (RF.K.2.a–2.e)	• *I Have…Who Has…? Interactive Game Cards* • *Word Building Cubes* • Index cards
	RF.1.2.b	Orally produce single-syllable words by blending sounds (phonemes), including consonant blends.	RF.K.2.b, RF.K.2.c	• *Word Building Cubes*
	RF.1.2.c	Isolate and pronounce initial, medial vowel, and final sounds (phonemes) in spoken single-syllable words.	RF.K.2.d	• *Word Building Cubes*
	RF.1.2.d	Segment spoken single-syllable words into their complete sequence of individual sounds (phonemes).	RF.K.2.e	• *Word Building Cubes*

*If your student has not met the prerequisite skills for this standard, drill down to the Kindergarten standard referenced here.

**Teaching Materials listed in italics are included in the kit; those not italicized are not included and can be found in your classroom.

English Language Arts

STRAND & CLUSTER	CCSS CODE	STANDARD	DRILL DOWN*	TEACHING MATERIALS**
STRAND: READING/FOUNDATIONAL SKILLS *(continued)*				
Phonics and Word Recognition	RF.1.3	Know and apply grade-level phonics and word analysis skills in decoding words.	RF.K.3 (RF.K.3.a–3.d)	*See:* RF.1.3.a, RF.1.3.b, RF.1.3.c, RF.1.3.d, RF.1.3.e, RF.1.3.f, RF.1.3.g
	RF.1.3.a	Know the spelling-sound correspondences for common consonant digraphs.	RF.K.3.a	• *Big Box of Word Chunks*
	RF.1.3.b	Decode regularly spelled one-syllable words.	RF.K.3 (RF.K.3.a–3.d)	• *Word Building Cubes* • *Big Box of Word Chunks*
	RF.1.3.c	Know final -e and common vowel team conventions for representing long vowel sounds.	RF.K.3 (RF.K.3.a–3.d)	• *Word Building Cubes*
	RF.1.3.d	Use knowledge that every syllable must have a vowel sound to determine the number of syllables in a printed word.	RF.K.3 (RF.K.3.a–3.d)	• *SpinZone Magnetic Whiteboard Spinners* • *Write-on/Wipe-off Crayons*
	RF.1.3.e	Decode two-syllable words following basic patterns by breaking the words into syllables.	RF.K.3 (RF.K.3.a–3.d)	• *Word Building Cubes*
	RF.1.3.f	Read words with inflectional endings.	RF.K.3 (RF.K.3.a–3.d)	• *Graphic Organizer Flip Chart*
	RF.1.3.g	Recognize and read grade-appropriate irregularly spelled words.	RF.K.3 (RF.K.3.a–3.d)	• *SpinZone Magnetic Whiteboard Spinners* • *Write-on/Wipe-off Crayons*
Fluency	RF.1.4	Read with sufficient accuracy and fluency to support comprehension.	RF.K.4	• *See:* R.F.1.4.a, R.F.1.4.b, R.F.1.4.c
	RF.1.4.a	Read grade-level text with purpose and understanding.	RF.K.4	• *Graphic Organizer Flip Chart* • Classroom reading materials
	RF.1.4.b	Read grade-level text orally with accuracy, appropriate rate, and expression on successive readings.	RF.K.4	• *Retell a Story Cubes* • *Parts of a Story Thumball* • Storybooks or other classroom reading materials
	RF.1.4.c	Use context to confirm or self-correct word recognition and understanding, rereading as necessary.	RF.K.4	• Storybooks or other classroom reading materials

*If your student has not met the prerequisite skills for this standard, drill down to the Kindergarten standard referenced here.

**Teaching Materials listed in italics are included in the kit; those not italicized are not included and can be found in your classroom.

English Language Arts

STRAND & CLUSTER	CCSS CODE	STANDARD	DRILL DOWN*	TEACHING MATERIALS**
STRAND: WRITING				
Text Types and Purposes	W.1.1	Write opinion pieces in which they introduce the topic or name the book they are writing about, state an opinion, supply a reason for the opinion, and provide some sense of closure.	W.K.1	• *Graphic Organizer Flip Chart* • Handwriting paper/student notebooks • Classroom reading materials
	W.1.2	Write informative/explanatory texts in which they name a topic, supply some facts about the topic, and provide some sense of closure.	W.K.2	• *Writing Prompts Cards* • *Graphic Organizer Flip Chart* • Handwriting paper/student notebooks
	W.1.3	Write narratives in which they recount two or more appropriately sequenced events, include some details regarding what happened, use temporal words to signal event order, and provide some sense of closure.	W.K.3	• *Speaker's Box* • Handwriting paper/student notebooks
Production and Distribution of Writing	W.1.4	(W.1.4 begins in grade 3)	N/A	N/A
	W.1.5	With guidance and support from adults, focus on a topic, respond to questions and suggestions from peers, and add details to strengthen writing as needed.	W.K.5	• *Writing Prompts Cards* • *Graphic Organizer Flip Chart* • Handwriting paper/student notebooks
	W.1.6	With guidance and support from adults, use a variety of digital tools to produce and publish writing, including in collaboration with peers.	W.K.6	• Computers, tablets, cameras
Research to Build and Present Knowledge	W.1.7	Participate in shared research and writing projects (e.g., explore a number of "how-to" books on a given topic and use them to write a sequence of instructions).	W.K.7	• *Writing Prompts Cards* • *Graphic Organizer Flip Chart* • Handwriting paper/student notebooks
	W.1.8	With guidance and support from adults, recall information from experiences or gather information from provided sources to answer a question.	W.K.8	• *Writing Prompts Cards* • *Graphic Organizer Flip Chart* • Handwriting paper/student notebooks
	W.1.9	(W.1.9 begins in grade 4)	N/A	N/A
Range of Writing	W.1.10	(W.1.10 begins in grade 3)	N/A	N/A

*If your student has not met the prerequisite skills for this standard, drill down to the Kindergarten standard referenced here.

**Teaching Materials listed in italics are included in the kit; those not italicized are not included and can be found in your classroom.

English Language Arts

STRAND & CLUSTER	CCSS CODE	STANDARD	DRILL DOWN*	TEACHING MATERIALS**
STRAND: SPEAKING AND LISTENING				
Comprehension and Collaboration	SL.1.1	Participate in collaborative conversations with diverse partners about *grade 1 topics and texts* with peers and adults in small and larger groups.	SL.K.1 (SL.K.1.a–1.b)	*See:* SL.1.1.a, SL.1.1.b, SL.1.1.c
	SL.1.1.a	Follow agreed-upon rules for discussions (e.g., listening to others with care, speaking one at a time about the topics and texts under discussion).	SL.K.1.a	• Pictures from the newspaper, magazines, or classroom activities
	SL.1.1.b	Build on others' talk in conversations by responding to the comments of others through multiple exchanges.	SL.K.1.b	• *Speaker's Box*
	SL.1.1.c	Ask questions to clear up any confusion about the topics and texts under discussion.	SL.K.1.b, SL.K.2, SL.K.3	• *Speaker's Box* • Classroom reading materials • Pictures from newspapers or other sources
	SL.1.2	Ask and answer questions about key details in a text read aloud or information presented orally or through other media.	SL.K.2	• *Talking in Sentences* • *SpinZone Magnetic Whiteboard Spinners* • Classroom reading materials
	SL.1.3	Ask and answer questions about what a speaker says in order to gather additional information or clarify something that is not understood.	SL.K.3	• *Speaker's Box* • Appendix B: Encouraging Social Interactions and Conversations
Presentation of Knowledge and Ideas	SL.1.4	Describe people, places, things, and events with relevant details, expressing ideas and feelings clearly.	SL.K.4	• *Talking in Sentences* • *Speaker's Box* • Classroom reading materials • Pictures of familiar people, places, things, or events from the student's life
	SL.1.5	Add drawings or other visual displays to descriptions when appropriate to clarify ideas, thoughts, and feelings.	SL.K.5	• Classroom art supplies such as paper, pencils, and crayons
	SL.1.6	Produce complete sentences when appropriate to task and situation.	SL.K.6	• *Talking in Sentences*

*If your student has not met the prerequisite skills for this standard, drill down to the Kindergarten standard referenced here.

**Teaching Materials listed in italics are included in the kit; those not italicized are not included and can be found in your classroom.

English Language Arts

STRAND & CLUSTER	CCSS CODE	STANDARD	DRILL DOWN*	TEACHING MATERIALS**
STRAND: LANGUAGE				
Conventions of Standard English	L.1.1	Demonstrate command of the conventions of standard English grammar and usage when writing or speaking.	L.K.1 (L.K.1.a – 1.f)	*See:* L.1.1.a, L.1.1.b, L.1.1.c, L.1.1.d, L.1.1.e, L.1.1.f, L.1.1.g, L.1.1.h, L.1.1.i, L.1.1.j
	L.1.1.a	Print all upper- and lowercase letters.	L.K.1.a	• Classroom handwriting paper and writing utensils
	L.1.1.b	Use common, proper, and possessive nouns.	L.K.1.b	• *Writing Prompts Cards* • Classroom reading materials
	L.1.1.c	Use singular and plural nouns with matching verbs in basic sentences (e.g., He hops; We hop).	L.K.1.c	• *Sentence Building Dominoes* • *Talking in Sentences* • *Speaker's Box* • *Writing Prompts Cards*
	L.1.1.d	Use personal, possessive, and indefinite pronouns (e.g., I, me, my; they, them, their, anyone, everything).	L.K.1.b, L.K.1.c	• *Talking in Sentences* • *Sentence Building Dominoes* • *SpinZone Magnetic Whiteboard Spinners* • *Writing Prompts Cards* • *Write-on/Wipe-off Crayons*
	L.1.1.e	Use verbs to convey a sense of past, present, and future (e.g., Yesterday I walked home; Today I walk home; Tomorrow I will walk home).	L.K.1.b	• *SpinZone Magnetic Whiteboard Spinners* • *Write-on/Wipe-off Crayons* • *Talking in Sentences* • *Sentence Building Dominoes*
	L.1.1.f	Use frequently occurring adjectives.	L.K.1.b	• *SpinZone Magnetic Whiteboard Spinners* • *Write-on/Wipe-off Crayons* • *Sentence Building Dominoes* • *Talking in Sentences* • *Writing Prompts Cards*
	L.1.1.g	Use frequently occurring conjunctions (e.g., *and, but, or, so, because*).	L.K.1.b, L.K.1.f	• *Sentence Building Dominoes*
	L.1.1.h	Use determiners (e.g., articles, demonstratives).	L.K.1.b, L.K.1.f	• *Speaker's Box* • *Sentence Building Dominoes* • *SpinZone Magnetic Whiteboard Spinners* • *Writing Prompts Cards*
	L.1.1.i	Use frequently occurring prepositions (e.g., *during, beyond, toward*).	L.K.1.e	• *Talking in Sentences* • *SpinZone Magnetic Whiteboard Spinners* • *Write-on/Wipe-off Crayons* • *Sentence Building Dominoes*

*If your student has not met the prerequisite skills for this standard, drill down to the Kindergarten standard referenced here.

**Teaching Materials listed in italics are included in the kit; those not italicized are not included and can be found in your classroom.

English Language Arts

STRAND & CLUSTER	CCSS CODE	STANDARD	DRILL DOWN*	TEACHING MATERIALS**
STRAND: LANGUAGE *(continued)*				
Conventions of Standard English *(continued)*	L.1.1.j	Produce and expand complete simple and compound declarative, interrogative, imperative, and exclamatory sentences in response to prompts.	L.K.1.f	• *Speaker's Box* • *Sentence Building Dominoes* • *Writing Prompts Cards*
	L.1.2	Demonstrate command of the conventions of standard English capitalization, punctuation, and spelling when writing.	L.K.2 (L.K.2.a–2.d)	*See:* L.1.2.a, L.1.2.b, L.1.2.c, L.1.2.d, L.1.2.e
	L.1.2.a	Capitalize dates and names of people.	L.K.2.a	• Index cards, paper
	L.1.2.b	Use end punctuation for sentences.	L.K.2.b	• *SpinZone Magnetic Whiteboard Spinners* • *Write-on/Wipe-off Crayons* • *Sentence Building Dominoes* • *Speaker's Box* • *Writing Prompts Cards*
	L.1.2.c	Use commas in dates and to separate single words in a series.	L.K.2.b	• Sentence strips, macaroni, glue
	L.1.2.d	Use conventional spelling for words with common spelling patterns and for frequently occurring irregular words.	L.K.2.c, L.K.2.d	• *Word Building Cubes* • *Big Box of Word Chunks*
	L.1.2.e	Spell untaught words phonetically, drawing on phonemic awareness and spelling conventions.	L.K.2.c, L.K.2.d	• *Big Box of Word Chunks* • *Word Building Cubes*
Knowledge of Language	L.1.3	(L.1.3 begins in grade 2)	N/A	N/A
Vocabulary Acquisition and Use	L.1.4	Determine or clarify the meaning of unknown and multiple-meaning words and phrases based on *grade 1 reading and content*, choosing flexibly from an array of strategies.	L.K.4 (L.K.4.a–4.b)	*See:* L.1.4.a, L.1.4.b, L.1.4.c
	L.1.4.a	Use sentence-level context as a clue to the meaning of a word or phrase.	L.K.4.a	• Classroom reading materials • Sentence strips • Index cards
	L.1.4.b	Use frequently occurring affixes as a clue to the meaning of a word.	L.K.4.b	• *SpinZone Magnetic Whiteboard Spinners* • Index cards • Sentence strips

*If your student has not met the prerequisite skills for this standard, drill down to the Kindergarten standard referenced here.

**Teaching Materials listed in italics are included in the kit; those not italicized are not included and can be found in your classroom.

English Language Arts

STRAND & CLUSTER	CCSS CODE	STANDARD	DRILL DOWN*	TEACHING MATERIALS**
STRAND: LANGUAGE *(continued)*				
Vocabulary Acquisition and Use *(continued)*	L.1.4.c	Identify frequently occurring root words (e.g., *look*) and their inflectional forms (e.g., *looks, looked, looking*).	L.K.4.b	• *Sentence Building Dominoes* • *SpinZone Magnetic Whiteboard Spinners* • *Talking in Sentences*
	L.1.5	With guidance and support from adults, demonstrate understanding of word relationships and nuances in word meanings.	L.K.5 (L.K.5.a–5.d)	*See:* L.1.5.a, L.1.5.b, L.1.5.c, L.1.5.d
	L.1.5.a	Sort words into categories (e.g., colors, clothing) to gain a sense of the concepts the categories represent.	L.K.5.a	• *SpinZone Magnetic Whiteboard Spinners* • *Sentence Building Dominoes* • Index cards
	L.1.5.b	Define words by category and by one or more key attributes (e.g., a *duck* is a bird that swims; a *tiger* is a large cat with stripes).	L.K.5.a	• *Sentence Building Dominoes* • *Talking in Sentences* • *Big Box of Word Chunks* • *SpinZone Magnetic Whiteboard Spinners* • Pictures from classroom books or other materials
	L.1.5.c	Identify real-life connections between words and their use (e.g., note places at home that are *cozy*).	L.K.5.c	• *Big Box of Word Chunks*
	L.1.5.d	Distinguish shades of meaning among verbs differing in manner (e.g., *look, peek, glance, stare, glare, scowl*) and adjectives differing in intensity (e.g., *large, gigantic*) by defining or choosing them or by acting out the meanings.	L.K.5.d	• *SpinZone Magnetic Whiteboard Spinners* • *Write-on/Wipe-off Crayons* • Index cards
	L.1.6	Use words and phrases acquired through conversations, reading and being read to, and responding to texts, including using frequently occurring conjunctions to signal simple relationships (e.g., *because*).	L.K.6	• Classroom reading materials • Visual, textual, or gestural prompts during conversation

*If your student has not met the prerequisite skills for this standard, drill down to the Kindergarten standard referenced here.

**Teaching Materials listed in italics are included in the kit; those not italicized are not included and can be found in your classroom.

Mathematics

DOMAIN & CLUSTER	CCSS CODE	STANDARD	DRILL DOWN*	TEACHING MATERIALS**
DOMAIN: OPERATIONS AND ALGEBRAIC THINKING				
Represent and solve problems involving addition and subtraction.	1.OA.A.1	Use addition and subtraction within 20 to solve word problems involving situations of adding to, taking from, putting together, taking apart, and comparing, with unknowns in all positions, e.g., by using objects, drawings, and equations with a symbol for the unknown number to represent the problem.[1] [1]See Mathematics Glossary Table 1 on page X.	K.OA.A.1	• Unifix Cubes • Working with Ten-Frames • Mathematics with Unifix Cubes • Ten-Frame Trains • Make a Splash 120 Mat Floor Game
	1.OA.A.2	Solve word problems that call for addition of three whole numbers whose sum is less than or equal to 20, e.g., by using objects, drawings, and equations with a symbol for the unknown number to represent the problem.	K.OA.A.2	• Working with Ten-Frames • Ten-Frame Trains • Unifix Cubes • Mathematics with Unifix Cubes • Thinking Mats
Understand and apply properties of operations and the relationship between addition and subtraction.	1.OA.B.3	Apply properties of operations as strategies to add and subtract.[2] Examples: If 8 + 3 = 11 is known, then 3 + 8 = 11 is also known. (Commutative property of addition.) To add 2 + 6 + 4, the second two numbers can be added to make a ten, so 2 + 6 + 4 = 2 + 10 = 12. (Associative property of addition.) [2]Students need not use formal terms for these properties.	K.OA.A.1, K.OA.A.3	• Thinking Mats • Write-on/Wipe-off Crayons • Ten-Frame Trains • Working with Ten-Frames
	1.OA.B.4	Understand subtraction as an unknown-addend problem. For example, subtract 10 – 8 by finding the number that makes 10 when added to 8.	K.OA.A.3	• Mathematics with Unifix Cubes • Unifix Cubes • Ten-Frame Trains • Working with Ten-Frames • Make a Splash 120 Mat Floor Game

*If your student has not met the prerequisite skills for this standard, drill down to the Kindergarten standard referenced here.

**Teaching Materials listed in italics are included in the kit; those not italicized are not included and can be found in your classroom.

Mathematics

DOMAIN & CLUSTER	CCSS CODE	STANDARD	DRILL DOWN*	TEACHING MATERIALS**
DOMAIN: OPERATIONS AND ALGEBRAIC THINKING *(continued)*				
Add and subtract within 20.	1.OA.C.5	Relate counting to addition and subtraction (e.g., by counting on 2 to add 2).	K.OA.A.1, K.OA.A.3	• *120 Number Mats* • *Write-on/Wipe-off Crayons* • *Ten-Frame Trains* • *Working with Ten-Frames* • *Unifix Cubes*
	1.OA.C.6	Add and subtract within 20, demonstrating fluency for addition and subtraction within 10. Use strategies such as counting on; making ten (e.g., 8 + 6 = 8 + 2 + 4 = 10 + 4 = 14); decomposing a number leading to a ten (e.g., 13 – 4 = 13 – 3 – 1 = 10 – 1 = 9); using the relationship between addition and subtraction (e.g., knowing that 8 + 4 = 12, one knows 12 – 8 = 4); and creating equivalent but easier or known sums (e.g., adding 6 + 7 by creating the known equivalent 6 + 6 + 1 = 12 + 1 = 13).	K.OA.A.1, K.OA.A.3, K.OA.A.5	• *Working with Ten-Frames* • *Ten-Frame Trains* • *Unifix Cubes* • *Mathematics with Unifix Cubes*
Work with addition and subtraction equations.	1.OA.D.7	Understand the meaning of the equal sign, and determine if equations involving addition and subtraction are true or false. For example, which of the following equations are true and which are false? 6 = 6, 7 = 8 – 1, 5 + 2 = 2 + 5, 4 + 1 = 5 + 2.	K.OA.A.1, K.OA.A.4	• *Thinking Mats* • *Write-On/Wipe-off Crayons* • *Unifix Cubes* • *Mathematics with Unifix Cubes*
	1.OA.D.8	Determine the unknown whole number in an addition or subtraction equation relating three whole numbers. For example, determine the unknown number that makes the equation true in each of the equations 8 + ? = 11, 5 = _ – 3, 6 + 6 = _.	K.OA.A.2, K.OA.A.3, K.OA.A.4	• *Make a Splash 120 Mat Floor Game* • *Unifix Cubes* • *Mathematics with Unifix Cubes* • *Thinking Mats*

*If your student has not met the prerequisite skills for this standard, drill down to the Kindergarten standard referenced here.
**Teaching Materials listed in italics are included in the kit; those not italicized are not included and can be found in your classroom.

Mathematics

DOMAIN & CLUSTER	CCSS CODE	STANDARD	DRILL DOWN*	TEACHING MATERIALS**
DOMAIN: NUMBER AND OPERATIONS IN BASE TEN				
Extend the counting sequence.	1.NBT.A.1	Count to 120, starting at any number less than 120. In this range, read and write numerals and represent a number of objects with a written numeral.	K.CC.A.1, K.CC.A.2, K.NBT.A.1	• *Make A Splash 120 Mat Floor Game* • *120 Number Mats* • *Write-on/Wipe-off Crayons*
Understand place value.	1.NBT.B.2	Understand that the two digits of a two-digit number represent amounts of tens and ones. Understand the following as special cases:	K.NBT.A.1	*See:* 1.NBT.B.2.a, 1.NBT.B.2.b, 1.NBT.B.2.c
	1.NBT.B.2.a	10 can be thought of as a bundle of ten ones—called a "ten."	K.NBT.A.1	• *Unifix Cubes* • *Ten-Frame Trains*
	1.NBT.B.2.b	The numbers from 11 to 19 are composed of a ten and one, two, three, four, five, six, seven, eight, or nine ones.	K.CC.B.5, K.NBT.A.1	• *Ten-Frame Trains* • *Unifix Cubes* • *Working with Ten-Frames* • Index Cards
	1.NBT.B.2.c	The numbers 10, 20, 30, 40, 50, 60, 70, 80, 90 refer to one, two, three, four, five, six, seven, eight, or nine tens (and 0 ones).	K.NBT.A.1	• *Unifix Cubes* • *120 Number Mats* • *Write-on/Wipe-off Crayons* • *Thinking Mats*
	1.NBT.B.3	Compare two two-digit numbers based on meanings of the tens and ones digits, recording the results of comparisons with the symbols >, =, and <.	K.CC.C.7, K.NBT.A.1	• *Mathematics with Unifix Cubes* • *Unifix Cubes* • *Thinking Mats* • *Ten-Frame Trains*

*If your student has not met the prerequisite skills for this standard, drill down to the Kindergarten standard referenced here.

**Teaching Materials listed in italics are included in the kit; those not italicized are not included and can be found in your classroom.

Mathematics

DOMAIN & CLUSTER	CCSS CODE	STANDARD	DRILL DOWN*	TEACHING MATERIALS**
DOMAIN: NUMBER AND OPERATIONS IN BASE TEN *(continued)*				
Use place value understanding and properties of operations to add and subtract.	1.NBT.C.4	Add within 100, including adding a two-digit number and a one-digit number, and adding a two-digit number and a multiple of 10, using concrete models or drawings and strategies based on place value, properties of operations, and/or the relationship between addition and subtraction; relate the strategy to a written method and explain the reasoning used. Understand that in adding two-digit numbers, one adds tens and tens, ones and ones; and sometimes it is necessary to compose a ten.	K.OA.A.1, K.NBT.A.1	• *Unifix Cubes* • *Mathematics with Unifix Cubes* • *120 Number Mats* • *Write-on/Wipe-off Crayons* • *Make a Splash 120 Mat Floor Game* • *Ten-Frame Trains* • *Thinking Mats* • Index cards • Timer
	1.NBT.C.5	Given a two-digit number, mentally find 10 more or 10 less than the number, without having to count; explain the reasoning used.	K.NBT.A.1	• *Make a Splash 120 Mat Floor Game* • *Ten-Frame Trains*
	1.NBT.C.6	Subtract multiples of 10 in the range 10-90 from multiples of 10 in the range 10-90 (positive or zero differences), using concrete models or drawings and strategies based on place value, properties of operations, and/or the relationship between addition and subtraction; relate the strategy to a written method and explain the reasoning used.	K.OA.A.1, K.OA.A.2, K.NBT.A.1	• *Working with Ten-Frames* • *120 Number Mats* • *Write-on/Wipe-off Crayons* • *Unifix Cubes* • *Make a Splash 120 Mat Floor Game* • *Ten-Frame Trains* • *Thinking Mats*
DOMAIN: MEASUREMENT AND DATA				
Measure lengths indirectly and by iterating length units.	1.MD.A.1	Order three objects by length; compare the lengths of two objects indirectly by using a third object.	K.MD.A.1, K.MD.A.2	• *Unifix Cubes* • *Mathematics with Unifix Cubes* • *Thinking Mats*
	1.MD.A.2	Express the length of an object as a whole number of length units, by laying multiple copies of a shorter object (the length unit) end to end; understand that the length measurement of an object is the number of same-size length units that span it with no gaps or overlaps. *Limit to contexts where the object being measured is spanned by a whole number of length units with no gaps or overlaps.*	K.CC.C.6	• *Mathematics with Unifix Cubes* • *Unifix Cubes*

*If your student has not met the prerequisite skills for this standard, drill down to the Kindergarten standard referenced here.

**Teaching Materials listed in italics are included in the kit; those not italicized are not included and can be found in your classroom.

Mathematics

DOMAIN & CLUSTER	CCSS CODE	STANDARD	DRILL DOWN*	TEACHING MATERIALS**
DOMAIN: MEASUREMENT AND DATA *(continued)*				
Tell and write time.	1.MD.B.3	Tell and write time in hours and half-hours using analog and digital clocks.	K.CC.A.1	• *Write-on/Wipe-off Clock Boards* • *Write-on/Wipe-off Crayons* • *Thinking Mats*
Represent and interpret data.	1.MD.C.4	Organize, represent, and interpret data with up to three categories; ask and answer questions about the total number of data points, how many in each category, and how many more or less are in one category than in another.	K.MD.B.3	• *Thinking Mats* • *Unifix Cubes* • *Mathematics with Unifix Cubes*
DOMAIN: GEOMETRY				
Reason with shapes and their attributes.	1.G.A.1	Distinguish between defining attributes (e.g., triangles are closed and three-sided) versus non-defining attributes (e.g., color, orientation, overall size); build and draw shapes to possess defining attributes.	K.G.A.1, K.G.A.2	• *Match It! Shape Shuffle* • *Thinking Mats*
	1.G.A.2	Compose two-dimensional shapes (rectangles, squares, trapezoids, triangles, half-circles, and quarter-circles) or three-dimensional shapes (cubes, right rectangular prisms, right circular cones, and right circular cylinders) to create a composite shape, and compose new shapes from the composite shape.[1] [1]Students should apply the principle of transitivity of measurement to make indirect comparisons, but they need not use this technical term.	K.G.A.3, K.G.B.4, K.G.B.5	• *Thinking Mats* • *Match It! Shape Shuffle*
	1.G.A.3	Partition circles and rectangles into two and four equal shares, describe the shares using the words *halves*, *fourths*, and *quarters*, and use the phrases *half of*, *fourth of*, and *quarter of*. Describe the whole as two of, or four of the shares. Understand for these examples that decomposing into more equal shares creates smaller shares.	K.G.A.1, K.G.A.2, K.G.B.6	• *Match It! Shape Shuffle* • *Thinking Mats*

*If your student has not met the prerequisite skills for this standard, drill down to the Kindergarten standard referenced here.

**Teaching Materials listed in italics are included in the kit; those not italicized are not included and can be found in your classroom.

Mathematics

MATHEMATICS GLOSSARY TABLE 1

COMMON ADDITION AND SUBTRACTION[1]			
	RESULT UNKNOWN	**CHANGE UNKNOWN**	**START UNKNOWN**
ADD TO	Two bunnies sat on the grass. Three more bunnies hopped there. How many bunnies are on the grass now? $2 + 3 = ?$	Two bunnies were sitting on the grass. Some more bunnies hopped there. Then there were five bunnies. How many bunnies hopped over to the first two? $2 + ? = 5$	Some bunnies were sitting on the grass. Three more bunnies hopped there. Then there were five bunnies. How many bunnies were on the grass before? $? + 3 = 5$
TAKE FROM	Five apples were on the table. I ate two apples. How many apples are on the table now? $5 - 2 = ?$	Five apples were on the table. I ate some apples. Then there were three apples. How many apples did I eat? $5 - ? = 3$	Some apples were on the table. I ate two apples. Then there were three apples. How many apples were on the table before? $? - 2 = 3$
	TOTAL UNKNOWN	**ADDEND UNKNOWN**	**BOTH ADDENDS UNKNOWN**[2]
PUT TOGETHER/ TAKE APART[3]	Three red apples and two green apples are on the table. How many apples are on the table? $3 + 2 = ?$	Five apples are on the table. Three are red and the rest are green. How many apples are green? $3 + ? = 5, 5 - 3 = ?$	Grandma has five flowers. How many can she put in the red vase and how many in her blue vase? $5 = 0 + 5, 5 = 5 + 0$ $5 = 1 + 4, 5 = 4 + 1$ $5 = 2 + 3, 5 = 3 + 2$
COMPARE[4]	**DIFFERENCE UNKNOWN**	**BIGGER UNKNOWN**	**SMALLER UNKNOWN**
	("How many more?" version): Lucy has two apples. Julie has five apples. How many more apples does Julie have than Lucy? ("How many fewer?" version): Lucy has two apples. Julie has five apples. How many fewer apples does Lucy have than Julie? $2 + ? = 5, 5 - 2 = ?$	(Version with "more"): Julie has three more apples than Lucy. Lucy has two apples. How many apples does Julie have? (Version with "fewer"): Lucy has 3 fewer apples than Julie. Lucy has two apples. How many apples does Julie have? $2 + 3 = ?, 3 + 2 = ?$	(Version with "more"): Julie has three more apples than Lucy. Julie has five apples. How many apples does Lucy have? (Version with "fewer"): Lucy has 3 fewer apples than Julie. Julie has five apples. How many apples does Lucy have? $5 - 3 = ?, ? + 3 = 5$

[1] Adapted from Box 2-4 of Mathematics Learning in Early Childhood, National Research Council (2009, pp. 32, 33).

[2] These take apart situations can be used to show all the decompositions of a given number. The associated equations, which have the total on the left of the equal sign, help children understand that the = sign does not always mean, makes or results in but always does mean is the same number as.

[3] Either addend can be unknown, so there are three variations of these problem situations. Both addends Unknown is a productive extension of the basic situation, especially for small numbers less than or equal to 10.

[4] For the Bigger Unknown or Smaller Unknown situations, one version directs the correct operation (the version using more for the bigger unknown and using less for the smaller unknown). The other versions are more difficult.

How To Use This Curriculum

COMMON CORE STATE STANDARDS AND SPECIAL EDUCATION

The adoption of the Common Core State Standards has been a matter of constant debate since its introduction. While the Common Care State Standards are somewhat ambiguous with respect to students with special needs, the fact remains that teachers across the nation are required to implement these standards with limited or no access to effective teaching tools for doing so.

The standards include a 2-page document entitled "Application to Students with Disabilities," which states that "students with disabilities are a heterogeneous group... therefore, *how* these standards are taught and assessed is of the utmost importance in reaching this diverse group of students" (www.corestandards.org/assets/ CCSSonSWD-AT.pdf). It uses optimistic language about providing "an historic opportunity to improve access to rigorous academic content standards for students with disabilities."

But many special education teachers are not feeling so optimistic. While access to the standards themselves is available, instruction on how to help our students actually meet the standards is negligible. "Application to Students with Disabilities" briefly mentions that Universal Design for Learning (UDL), instructional accommodations, and assistive technology devices should be used to implement standards, but provides no guidance for what this actually looks like in the classroom. It suggests making accommodations without changing the standards, a suggestion that ignores the individual needs of many of our students.

The Common Core addresses the idea that we need to rigorously prepare ALL students for a successful college and work experience. However, many challenges that we face in special education are not addressed at all, such as the need to teach daily living skills and social skills. These fundamental skills are essential for meeting the goal of the Common Core.

And the goal is a good one. We want our students to be held to high standards, we want to teach them at the edge of their abilities, and we want to provide access to opportunities such as college and meaningful careers, but we need to address the underlying prerequisite skills that make that a

tenable goal. Acknowledging that "*how* these standards are taught and assessed is of the utmost importance" but neglecting to provide resources and tools to teach and assess is counterproductive to attaining these goals.

This guide aims to address the gap in resources: Equipping you with a companion curriculum that specifically addresses the learning needs of students with autism and other special needs, providing resources and teaching strategies for target skills in both ELA and Math, and supplying tips for generalization. This guide utilizes the principles of Applied Behavior Analysis (ABA), an evidence-based practice, to implement the Common Core Standards for first grade. While we have included teaching materials in the kit, the targets stand alone, allowing you to use a wide range of materials and supplies that you already have in your classroom.

APPLIED BEHAVIOR ANALYSIS

Applied Behavior Analysis, or ABA, is an empirically proven treatment method for working with individuals with autism and related disorders. Founded in B.F. Skinner's studies of behavior, it focuses on the use of motivation to help individuals achieve their full potential. For decades, ABA has been used to teach a wide range of skills to learners with developmental disabilities.

In 1987, O. Ivar Lovaas published a groundbreaking study about using ABA for young children with autism (Lovaas, 1987; McEachin, Smith, & Lovaas, 1993). "Each of the children in this early intensive intervention project had received several hundred tailored treatment programs and made major and lasting gains in intellectual, social, emotional, and educational skills. Further, nine of the children showed no diagnosable autism at the end of treatment, and eight of those maintained their typical functioning throughout elementary school" (Larsson & Wright, 2011).

While ABA is frequently associated with treating Autism Spectrum Disorders, the principles of ABA can be used to improve the quality of education for any child. Studies have shown that ABA has resulted in positive outcomes for individuals with Down Syndrome, intellectual disabilities, and developmental delays, as well as with individuals who exhibit maladaptive behaviors. ABA consists of many

How To Use This Curriculum

strategies that can be incredibly effective in any classroom that contains students with special needs. Below I have outlined a few of these strategies and provided information about how they relate to the materials contained in this kit.

Data Collection

Data collection should be an essential part of any teaching methodology, and is the very foundation of ABA. Taking data daily and graphing the information makes it possible to quickly see when your student is making progress and when you need to make a change in your teaching procedure. Your school or organization may have a required format for compiling and graphing data. However, we have included reproducible data sheets and graphing sheets for both individuals and for group work, as well as completed samples in Appendix C.

Prior to taking data on a student's progress, it's essential to get baseline data, or information about your student's current level of ability for that skill. Your school will likely have its own methods for attaining and recording baseline data. It is important that you take baseline data on more than one day to avoid making incorrect assumptions. For example, you may state that your student does not know the skill if you only assess the skill on one day in which he happened to have slept little the previous night. Or you may overestimate you student's skill level if you only ask one question and he happens to guess correctly.

For students in special education, it is especially important to maintain skills once they have been mastered. Maintenance is the ability to continue performing the skill after intensive teaching has been completed. I have found it helpful to create index cards with mastered skills written so I can quickly go through maintenance tasks during classroom time. For example, an index card might say "names the letter 'A'" or "counts up to three objects." Failure to maintain previously mastered skills may result in the student losing those skills, thus requiring you to take time to reteach.

There are several methods for taking and displaying data. Here are brief descriptions of the most common types of data you may collect and when to use them.

Per Opportunity is a simple type of data collection that is used to record a student's performance on a task you are teaching. Each time the student has an opportunity to respond to the target demand, record a Yes (Y) or No (N). At the completion of the lesson, calculate the percentage of correct responses. If you are working with a group of students, use the *Per Opportunity Group Data Sheet*; if you are working with a student one-on-one, use the *Per Opportunity Individual Data Sheet* included in Appendix C.

Single-Probe is another form of data you can collect to record student progress in attaining new target skills. Record a plus (+) or minus (-) for only the first possible opportunity a student has to respond to a target demand. Though you only record data for the first possible opportunity, you provide multiple opportunities to practice the skill. If the student responds correctly on three consecutive days, the skill is considered mastered. On the one hand, this method can be beneficial for classroom teachers because the data collection is more manageable, but it does not provide as much information as Per Opportunity data.

ABC Data is used to determine the function of a student's behavior. It is a simple chart you can easily create that is divided into four columns:

- Date/time

- Antecedent — what happens directly before the behavior

- Behavior — what happened, described in a way that is *observable* (i.e., "dropped to the floor and screamed" instead of "tantrummed") and *measureable* (i.e., "screamed for 5 minutes")

- Consequence — what happened directly following the behavior (i.e., "student removed from room" or "teacher went to student's desk and helped him with the math problem")

A pattern may emerge in the consequence column, providing information about what is maintaining the behavior. For example, if you find that following most undesirable behaviors, the student is removed from the class, it is likely that this "time out" is maintaining the behavior.

Time Sampling is "a measurement of the presence or absence of behavior within specific time intervals" (Cooper et al., 2007). Time sampling is an effective way to collect data on continuous or high-rate behaviors. It is especially useful for behaviors that do not have a clear beginning or end, such as humming or repetitive behaviors. For time sampling, it's helpful to use a *MotivAider*, a simple electronic device that silently vibrates at timed intervals. It can be programmed to vibrate on a fixed or variable schedule at different duration and intensity levels. It allows you to collect data you otherwise wouldn't be able to while teaching because you don't have to keep an eye on the clock.

Task Analysis is used to collect accurate data for multi-step tasks. Break a larger task into smaller steps and record a plus (+) or minus (–) for the student's independent response to each step within the larger task. You can then divide the number the student completed successfully by the total number of steps to attain a percentage for correct responding for the total task. Task Analysis is frequently used for functional living skills such as washing hands or making a snack. You will find both a blank and a completed Task Analysis in Appendix C to further guide you.

Tips for Managing Data Collection in the Classroom Setting

All of the data that you collect can be used to make teaching decisions, as well as to accurately report information on Individualized Education Plans (IEPs), quarterly progress reports, and in annual reviews. Many teachers struggle with data collection in the classroom setting but it's not as difficult as it may seem to take data and maintain student attention in a busy classroom. Here are a few tips to help you take accurate data:

- Attach the *Per Opportunity Group Data Sheet* to a clipboard to take data on target skills during a small group lesson. It's easier to track data if you're only managing ONE page of information.

- Use tools such as a tally counter to take data for one student during a lesson. A small counter is great because you can put yarn through it and wear it around your neck.

- Place an address label or sticker on your pants or arm. You can mark tallies with a pen there as you teach without having to carry a clipboard or other materials.

- For some lessons, it may be challenging to take the data you need while teaching. Utilize your paraprofessional or assistant teachers. Give clear instructions on the target skill and what type of data you are seeking.

- Consider having your students help with data. You can have them put checkmarks or stickers in a box on an index card when you instruct them to. Collect the index cards at the end of the lesson to record the data.

- Keep it simple! Don't try to take too much data, as it will increase likelihood of errors. Consider simple yes/no data.

- Analyze your data! Your data is meaningless if you don't use it.

Definitions of Procedure and Mastery Criterion

Now that you understand the importance of data and how to take it in the classroom setting, let's take a look at what you do with that data. For each program that you are working on with your student, you should be taking daily data. The procedure for collecting that data and criterion for mastery are described in detail below.

Procedure & Data Collection

An opportunity—also called a trial—refers to a single opportunity to respond to the target question. For "Per Opportunity" data, you should record a 'Y' for a correct response and an 'N' for an incorrect response, prompted response, or no response. Divide the number of correct responses by the total number of opportunities, and you will have a percentage of correct responses, which can then be graphed on the *Per Opportunity Graph* in Appendix C. Per opportunity data can be collected in 1:1 teaching or in small group teaching. Appendix C contains both a *Per Opportunity Individual Data Sheet* and a *Per Opportunity Group Data Sheet.*

Mastery Criterion

Mastery criterion for Per Opportunity data is listed as 80% across three consecutive sessions with two different instructors. There is a *Per Opportunity Graph* in Appendix C for you to complete based on your needs. For example, there are rare instances in which you might want a student to have 100% accuracy, such as looking both ways before crossing the street or urinating in the toilet. You may also be in a teaching environment in which you don't have access to a second instructor, so your mastery criterion may be set for 80% across three consecutive sessions with one instructor. For the purposes of data collection in this curriculum kit, we have set mastery at 80%.

Preference Assessment

Conducting a Preference Assessment for each student should be one of the first things you do when you start teaching a student. You can find a complete *Preference Assessment* in Appendix A. Having a clear understanding of what items and activities are highly motivating for your student will provide opportunities to reinforce correct responses and adaptive behavior.

Having preferred items and activities available has several benefits:

1. It makes it easier for you to reinforce your student for correct responding and desirable behaviors.

2. It pairs you with preferred items, making teaching sessions more positive for the student.

3. It increases opportunities for the learner to request items because he/she will be more motivated to request the preferred items and activities you have made available.

To conduct a Preference Assessment, place many toys and objects within reach of the student and watch how he/she interacts with them for about 20-30 minutes. If you have a learner with poor scanning skills, you can present items two at a time and see what the learner reaches for.

Make several presentations of items to the student, arranging them in different groupings over the course of one session. As you are observing, make tally marks in the appropriate category on the *Preference Assessment* form to easily recognize patterns. When you have completed the assessment, fill in the final page to have a comprehensive list of reinforcing items and activities on record for that student. Conducting a Preference Assessment allows you to fully explore a range of potential items and activities, and also serves to remove your own bias. For example, not all kids are most motivated by the iPad; some kids may actually be most motivated by doing math flashcards.

When beginning a new session or lesson, you may want to informally assess your student's preferences. You can do this by simply asking, "What do you want to play with/ work for today?" or by placing items within reach and seeing what the student reaches for first.

Finally, it is important for you to get parent input. They may be aware of preferred items and activities that you had not previously considered. Parent reporting is also included in the *Preference Assessment* in Appendix A.

Pairing

If you are familiar with ABA, you have probably heard of the term "pairing." The idea behind pairing is that you will establish and maintain a positive relationship with the student by pairing yourself with preferred items or activities (yet another reason the Preference Assessment is so important). Pairing also helps maintain the relationship, prevent boredom, and increase motivation throughout your relationship with the student.

Before each lesson, you should engage in "pre-session" pairing. This means that you are providing free reinforcers without placing demands. For early learners, you might start off a session with blowing bubbles or playing with a parachute. For older learners, you might start off a session with a game or sharing a book the student enjoys. In the classroom, this might include singing a favorite song or giving high-fives as the students take their seats. If possible, it's a good idea to present the students with options during pre-session pairing. Involving choice frequently increases motivation, and it also increases the likelihood of delivering a more highly reinforcing item.

You may feel that pairing every day eats up valuable instructional time. However, pre-session pairing actually serves to increase motivation and cuts down on maladaptive behavior, which increases the amount and the quality of your instructional time for a given lesson (Rispoli et al., 2011).

Variety and novelty are important during pairing as well. A common error is using the same pre-session pairing with every learner. What you believe is reinforcing in general may not be reinforcing for your student in particular. By completing a Preference Assessment, you can avoid this error.

How To Use This Curriculum

Another common error is using the same pre-session pairing items and activities for every session. A student may love singing "Row Your Boat" one session, and then have no interest the next session. Or, what I see much more often, the learner may love singing "Row Your Boat" every day for two months, and then suddenly has no interest in it. The teacher has depended too heavily on this one preferred activity. Then, without a powerful reinforcer to pair with and use throughout the session, the learner displays a drop in motivation and sometimes a correlating increase in maladaptive behaviors.

There's a word for this: *satiation*. Cooper et al. define satiation as: "A decrease in the frequency of operant behavior presumed to be the result of continued contact with or consumption of a reinforcer that has followed the behavior" (2007). Some students you work with may satiate on reinforcers within minutes, while others may prefer to see the same items over and over from session to session. A student's satiation can vary based on many different variables, so you should be prepared to address it.

One way to address this is to choose not to use the same reinforcers during each session. This way, if a battery dies, you run out of stickers, or something breaks, you have not set yourself and your student up for failure. A second way to address satiation is to remove the item or activity while the student is still highly motivated to engage with it, instead of waiting until he or she has lost interest before introducing other choices.

A final consideration is that students with autism and other developmental delays are frequently provided with sensory items that can be stretched, smooshed, or illuminated. While the items are certainly valuable for pairing and for reinforcement, it may be more valuable to engage in activities with the student, such as cause-and-effect toys and games, or physical activities that require your joint involvement.

Pairing is not an activity that can be easily measured, and it's important to recognize that the pairing process is never finished but is an ongoing part of your relationship with each student. When pairing is consistent, specific to students' interests, and involves a variety of items and activities, students will maintain motivation and you will be more easily able to maintain instructional control.

Motivation and Reinforcement

Reinforcement is a much more complicated subject than it initially appears to be. As previously mentioned, it is necessary to complete a Preference Assessment for each child to learn about what they find reinforcing prior to teaching. Here are a few important things to remember about reinforcement:

- Reinforcement should be individualized for your particular student. Some students are highly motivated by light-up toys or movement activities, others by edibles or music. Just because you think it is reinforcing does not mean that it is! If the learner is not engaging with the item by ignoring it, putting it down, or displaying maladaptive behaviors when the item is present, then the item is not reinforcing at that time.

- Reinforcement should be varied as much as possible. You do not want your student to satiate on the one item or activity that you use all the time for reinforcement.

- Reinforcement is most powerful when it is provided within one second of the desired response to the target question. The longer the amount of time between correct responding and reinforcement, the less meaningful the reinforcement, and the less likely your student is to connect reinforcement to the target response. Moreover, it potentially reinforces behavior that may have occurred in the interim.

- Use differential reinforcement. This means that you provide different qualities of reinforcement for different qualities of responses. For example, if your student answers quickly, clearly, and correctly on the first try you can provide a highly preferred reinforcer. But if your student answers correctly with a minimal prompt, you would provide a less preferred reinforcer. This is another time when access to the *Preference Assessment* results form is beneficial for the teacher because it provides a hierarchy of preferred reinforcers.

- You should work to establish new items as reinforcing, broadening the scope of reinforcers over time. Your ultimate goal is that your student becomes reinforced by your teaching materials or by events likely to occur in the natural environment such as playing chase on the playground or having a person smile at them.

- In order to prevent satiation, you should try to keep the preference list robust so that you can vary the reinforcement provided. Think about what happens if you're teaching and your student's preferred activity is watching YouTube on a tablet. If you have not worked with a broad range of preferred items and activities, then you're bound to have a very difficult lesson on the day your Wi-Fi isn't working.

- The pace of instruction and delivery of reinforcement should be fast.

Using Motivating Materials and Activities for Teaching

There are two important ways to use motivating materials and activities with your students. The first is to find highly engaging materials for teaching. For each Common Core State Standard, you will find multiple materials and activities in this kit for teaching and generalizing each skill, which increases the likelihood of having motivating materials available for each individual student. For example, for ELA.L.1.1.c, the standard states that the student will be able to "use singular and plural nouns with matching verbs in basic sentences." You will see that there are four different materials included in the kit that address that skill. If you know your student struggles with this skill, you should start by picking materials that have the highest likelihood of engaging your student. If your students loves blocks, you may start with the *Sentence Building Dominoes* because they provide an opportunity to manipulate and assemble words.

The second way to use motivating materials is as positive reinforcement for correct responses. Below is an example of what reinforcement might look like for Math.1.G.A.1. The target skill in this example is for the student to identify two or more defining attributes for at least eight shapes. In the chart below, the target skill is listed in bold. You'll see from the chart that the target skill is interspersed with mastered skills, such as naming the shape or counting with 1:1 correspondence. The student's most highly-preferred reinforcers are high-fives, stickers, and playing with puppets. Other reinforcers include singing a song, verbal praise, and squeezing a ball. The teacher refers to the student's *Preference Assessment* results to link reinforcement to the current lesson.

TASK	INSTRUCTOR SAYS	STUDENT RESPONSE	REINFORCEMENT
Identify the name of a shape	"What shape is this?"	"Triangle."	"That's right!"
Identify defining attribute	"How do you know it's a triangle?"	"It has three sides."	"It does have three sides!" combined with high five.
Identify second defining attribute	"What else tells you it's a triangle?"	"Because it has three sides."	No reinforcement: incorrect response, move to prompt
(Repeat) **Identify second defining attribute**	"I know it's a triangle because it has three sides *and it is*..." (provides gestural prompt for *closed* that was used in initial instruction.)	"Closed!"	"Good job."
Identify how many shapes are on the table	"How many shapes do you see?"	"Three shapes."	"That's right."
Identify the name of a shape	"What is the name of this shape?"	"It's a square."	"Nice work."
Identify defining attribute	"How do you know it's a square?"	"It has four sides all the same size."	"It is a square because it has four sides!" combined with a high five and the opportunity to choose a sticker.

For more information on reinforcement and using it effectively, I suggest having a look at *The NEW ABA Program Companion* by J. Tyler Fovel, M.A., BCBA.

How To Use This Curriculum

Discriminative Stimulus

Throughout this curriculum you will find the abbreviation 'Sd,' which stands for *discriminative stimulus*. Cooper et al. (2007) define discriminative stimulus as "a stimulus in the presence of which responses of some type have been reinforced and in the absence of which the same type of responses have occurred and not been reinforced." To put it in other terms, the *Sd* is what you say or do to evoke a response that you will reinforce. For example, when teaching a child to respond to "What is your name?" you may give them a high five, verbal praise, or other reinforcement when they respond correctly. The *Sd* in that example is your statement "What is your name?" For each program in the curriculum, we have provided several examples of an *Sd* so you are able to vary it, therefore decreasing the potential for rote responding.

Prompting

When teaching new skills, you may find that your student requires prompts. "A prompt is assistance given by the teacher to promote correct responding" (Leaf & McEachin, 1999). It is important to systematically fade prompts to avoid "prompt dependence" which is when a learner requires a prompt from a teacher or parent in order to complete a task.

There are many different ways to prompt which can be divided into levels according to how intrusive the prompt is. Below is a prompt hierarchy, with the least intrusive prompt at the top and the most intrusive prompt at the bottom. Your goal is to quickly progress through the prompt levels to move your learner to independence.

PROMPTING HIERARCHY

Research indicates that most-to-least prompting is most effective to teach new skills, whereas least-to-most prompting is preferred for maintaining skills the student has already learned. This means that when teaching a new skill, you would start at the most intrusive prompt, a full physical prompt, and then move your way up the prompt hierarchy until your learner achieves independence with the task.

In order to decrease the possibility of prompt dependence, you should try to quickly move up the prompt hierarchy in a way that makes sense for the skill you are trying to teach. Below are some tips to help you help your learners achieve independence:

- Follow the rule of three: Once your learner has successfully responded to a question three times consecutively, move to a less intrusive prompt.

- If you are taking data, make a notation of what prompt level you are using at each step. And remember: only independent responses should be counted towards the learner's percentage of correct responses.

- At the end of a session or group of trials, note what prompt level you were at by the end of the session. Then start at that level during the next session.

- If your learner does not respond correctly when you move to a less intrusive prompt, then move back to the most recent prompt level. Once they respond again correctly at that prompt level three times consecutively, move again to a less intrusive prompt.

- It's important to note that while verbal prompts are less intrusive than many other types of prompts, they are the most difficult to fade. Though they are less intrusive, you should avoid using them when possible.

- Write down what the prompt levels will look like for the specific task you are teaching in advance. This way you will be fully prepared to quickly move your learner towards independence.

- Differentiate your reinforcement! If you move to a less intrusive prompt and the learner responds correctly, then you should immediately provide a stronger reinforcer than you did for previous responses. If a learner spontaneously responds without a prompt, you should do what I call "throwing them a party" by combining reinforcers (such as tickles and high fives) or by providing a highly desirable reinforcer.

How To Use This Curriculum

- You can pair prompts and then fade out the more intrusive prompts. In the example of pulling up pants in the table below, you can pair a visual prompt with a gestural prompt by showing the symbol for pulling up pants while pointing at the pants. Over time, you stop using the gestural prompt and just use the symbol. You can fade the symbol by systematically making it smaller or fainter.

Below are two different examples illustrating each prompt level from least-to-most intrusive. In the first column, you'll find the prompt level. In the example given in the second column, the goal is for the learner to greet a person who walks into the room. In the example in the third column, the goal is for the learner to pull up his/her pants after using the bathroom as a part of a toileting routine.

PROMPT LEVEL	GREETING	PULLING UP PANTS
Natural Cue/Independence	Learner says "Hello" upon seeing person enter room.	Learner pulls up pants immediately after flushing or after wiping (whichever step is directly before "pulling up pants".)
Visual Prompt	It's possible that you may use some sort of textual prompt, then fade the script, such as showing the words "Hello, how are you today?"	You may have symbols or a picture schedule the student uses to remember the steps for toileting.
Verbal Prompt	You say, "Say Hello," then the learner says, "Hello."	You say, "What comes next?" or "Pull up your pants." Then the learner pulls them up without assistance.
Gestural Prompt	You silently point or nod toward the person who has entered the room, then the learner says, "Hello."	You point at the pants, and then the learner pulls them up without assistance.
Modeling	You say "Hello, _____" and wave, then the learner says, "Hello." You may include a prompt such as "Follow me" or "Do what I do."	N/A
Partial Physical Prompt	You might touch the learner's elbow and gently raise his/her hand to begin waving in greeting, and then let him/her finish the wave and say, "Hello."	You may tap or gently press the learner's wrist or elbows towards the floor, and then let him/her finish pulling up his/her pants.
Full Physical Prompt	You pick up the learner's hand and wave it in greeting.	You gently guide the learner's hands to pick up his/her pants, and then guide him/her through the process of pulling them up.

How To Use This Curriculum

Generalization

Many students with special needs struggle to generalize skills. We must address this in our teaching by ensuring that our students are able to successfully use a skill in all environments, with all people, and with all materials. Here are a few examples of what it may look like when a student has not generalized a skill:

- Has *not* generalized across environments: The student is able to accurately count groups of objects in the classroom but is unable to count out tokens to claim a prize at a fair.

- Has *not* generalized across people: The student will respond to "wh" questions when presented by the teacher during a lesson, but will not respond to "wh" questions when asked a question by the crossing guard on the way to school.

- Has *not* generalized across materials: The student can match pictured items but is unable to match socks when helping with laundry at home.

As you teach, it is essential to build in opportunities for generalization in each lesson. This kit includes materials and other suggestions for generalizing skills. In addition, the *Per Opportunity Graph* in Appendix C provides space for you to note the materials, people, and environments you used for both teaching and generalization to ensure the student is gaining full independence with the target skill.

Generalization Criterion

For each standard, it is important to conduct a generalization probe. This means you will present the demand with novel materials, in a novel environment, or by a novel person. The student has generalized the skill if they respond correctly on the first attempt. Information about your generalization probes can be recorded at the bottom of the *Per Opportunity Graph* in Appendix C. You should also record the date of the generalization probe in the appropriate column on the program pages.

Natural Environment Teaching (NET)

Beyond providing teaching opportunities during lessons individually or in small groups, you will also want to provide opportunities to respond to the target skill in the natural environment. The natural environment may include the playground, the grocery store, interactions with peers during free play, or any other area in which skills would be applied outside of the teaching environment. You should embed teaching targets into play scenarios, games, or activities.

NET is especially important for students with autism and other developmental delays who struggle with generalization. It is not useful for these children to only be capable of completing a task in a teaching session. Planning lessons that utilize skills in the natural environment is essential. For example, if you are working on the Common Core standards in the *Speaking and Listening* strand, it is not useful for a student to only be able to ask questions at the table in the classroom. Creating opportunities for students to be taught how to ask questions in the community, in stores, or during play is an important part of the teaching process.

CONSIDERATIONS AND RESOURCES RELATED TO LANGUAGE DEVELOPMENT

The Common Core State Standards include many requirements for students to share thoughts, speak in grammatically correct sentences, and provide appropriate conversational responses. While these expectations may be developmentally appropriate for their same-age peers, teaching language out of developmental order can have long-lasting counterproductive effects. For this reason, it is important to assess and understand each student's developmental skill in the area of language, then teach to their individual needs.

For additional information you should visit the website www.corestandards.org. The site includes detailed information about each standard, as well as research related to how the standards were made. For ELA standards, we highly recommend that you look at the Test Exemplars and Sample Performance Tasks found at www.corestandards.org/assets/Appendix_B.pdf, a document that provides dozens of suggested texts for a range of standards. This can be especially helpful as you are choosing appropriate reading materials for meeting the standards with your individual students.

How To Use This Curriculum

As a special education teacher, if you are working with children with autism or severe language delays, you should be aware of the stages of language development, assess your student's language ability, and set appropriate goals for the best long-term benefits of that student. *The Verbal Behavior Milestones Assessment and Placement Program* (VB-MAPP) by Mark Sundberg, PhD, is an excellent tool for assessing and setting goals for your students.

You can also utilize Brown's Stages of Language Development. It's important to note that while Brown lists the approximate ages that most children develop these language skills, it is essential to teach to the current *developmental stage* your student is in, and not their *chronological age*. You can find a sample of the Stages of Language Development at www.education.com/reference/article/acquisition-sentence-forms.

After you have assessed, you should refer to Appendix B, *Encouraging Social Interactions and Conversations*, for guidance on supporting your student at their current level of language development. This appendix provides suggestions for encouraging mands, as well as multiple examples of mands you can teach in the classroom environment. It will also provide examples of leading statements you can make to promote the skill of asking questions.

Frequently, teachers may feel pressure from parents, administrators, or other staff to teach language skills that are well above an individual student's current level of functioning. This can produce serious problems in the student's communication skills. For example, if you have a student who is in Stage 1 of Brown's Stages of Language Development, but you are requiring them to use full sentences to communicate, it's likely that they will not comprehend all of the words in the sentence. You may see errors such as these:

Teacher: What should I do?
Student: I want throw please.

Teacher: Do you want to draw or listen to music?
Student: Give me draw please.

While it may take much longer for our students to move through the stages than their typically developing peers, it is important that we meet them at their current skill level.

If you teach well above their current skill level, research shows that they do not acquire full comprehension of basic language, misuse common words, and/or plateau in their language development.

There are several special considerations a teacher must make when choosing how to practice communication effectively with students. Below I've outlined some common obstacles and potential teaching methods for addressing them.

Concern: When teaching language with discrete trials, it is possible that students may become prompt dependent and fail to initiate conversation on their own or participate in novel conversation.
Teaching Method: Utilize paraprofessionals, teaching assistants, and parents when possible to teach conversation. One adult should be the conversation partner who will discuss highly motivating topics with the student. The other adult will be responsible for all prompts. This way, the conversation maintains a natural form and cadence since one adult is solely responsible for prompting and doesn't have to converse.

Concern: For students who are not yet speaking, you need to provide opportunities for teaching the concept of social exchanges.
Teaching Method: You may use tools such as sign language, Picture Exchange Communication System, or an augmentative/alternative communication device.

Concern: Some students may struggle greatly with basic aspects of communication such as eye contact and orienting their body towards the conversation partner.
Teaching Method: These students need to be reinforced for these behaviors to increase the future frequency. For example, when a student makes eye contact, you can provide reinforcement such as high fives, silly faces or sounds, or access to tangibles. More importantly, communication and conversation should be individualized for each student, and it should be FUN! You can increase your student's interest by engaging them with activities and topics they are motivated by, using materials that encourage active play, and planning breaks as needed.

How To Use This Curriculum

Concern: For students struggling with communication, it's important to recognize that as a teacher, a pattern of reinforcing being quiet and waiting for instruction may actually decrease spontaneous vocalizations (Sundberg & Partington, 1999, pp. 139–156).

Teaching Method: Focus on reinforcing spontaneous vocalizations and babbling. Consider using activity schedules as a visual prompt for a learner to initiate a social interaction (McClannahan & Kranz, 2005, pp. 10–11).

While it is important to provide rigorous academic programs for our students, the unique concerns listed above make implementation of the Common Core State Standards challenging. The "Application for Students with Disabilities" discusses providing "meaningful access" to the standards. If we teach well above a student's current skill level, we are not providing meaningful access. Every first grade standard correlates with a kindergarten standard. If your student is unable to complete any of the tasks on one of the standards in this book, you can drill down to the correlated standard in the *ABA Curriculum for the Common Core: Kindergarten.* You can reference the Overview grid that provides the kindergarten standards associated with each first grade standard. You can also find this information on the bottom of each standard page. If you drill down to the kindergarten standard, but your student is still unable to complete the tasks for that standard, we recommend that you assess using the VB-MAPP. While your school may require you to use a different assessment (such as the SANDI), it is still useful to complete the VB-MAPP because it provides an accurate portrait of your student's current skill level and barriers to learning, as well as makes recommendations for appropriate IEP goals.

Below is a list of some possible signs that you may be teaching above your student's current skill level:

- The student masters a goal when taught in discrete trials, but has not mastered the prerequisite skills.

- After the student masters a skill, he/she is not able to maintain it if it is practiced with lower frequency.

- The student masters a skill but is unable to respond accurately when it is intermixed with other mastered skills.

- The student is unable to generalize the skill after mastery.

- The student is not mastering any of the material that you are teaching.

- The student is mastering one skill at a much slower rate than he/she typically masters skills.

It is absolutely imperative that you meet each student at his/her current skill level, even if that means you do not start with the CCSS. However, the use of the CCSS provides guidelines for the overall scope of what we want our students to learn, and it provides teaching opportunities within each standard.

How to Use This Kit

PUTTING IT ALL TOGETHER

This kit is specifically designed to address the English Language Arts and Math goals in the Common Core State Standards **for students in special education**. Each standard is broken down into small, teachable steps to help track student progress to make the CCSS accessible for students with special needs.

Each strand has an overview page denoting the standards, kit materials, additional classroom materials and activities, and a tip for generalization. This is followed by individual pages for each Common Core State Standard enabling you to take data on when the target was introduced, mastered and generalized directly on the page for each student. The standard pages also provide detailed information on teaching procedure, how to use the materials in that particular lesson, along with the discriminative stimulus used for that target skill.

You should start by exploring the teaching materials contained within the kit. Think about how you might use them to meet your students' current needs. Ask yourself:

- What might be highly motivating for each student?

- What materials would be best for independent work? Group work?

- Are there any materials that might be aversive to particular students?

- What areas of the classroom would be best for setting up or storing these materials?

- How can I use the materials in conjunction with the materials I already have in the classroom?

Once you're comfortable with the scope of the materials, familiarize yourself with the curriculum book and how each standard is organized. Every page in this kit is designed to be reproducible for each student in your classroom. Everything you need to teach and record information about student progress is contained within this book and can be taught with the included kit materials. However, the targets can also be used independently with any teaching materials or activities that may be appropriate for a particular student.

We have intentionally selected materials for this kit to mutually support different targets. While we highlight one or two specific materials explained in depth in the Teaching Procedure, we also list additional kit materials that can be used to teach, maintain or generalize the target skills in each program.

While we do our best to include the exact products described in the Teaching Procedure, there may be rare occasions when a product is unavailable for an extended period of time or has been suddenly discontinued. In these cases, we will substitute the product with one of equal purpose and value that you can still use for the Teaching Procedure described.

The sample pages that follow will serve as a User Guide to the salient information presented on each Strand and Standard page.

Strand Reference Page

Brief description of the skill set addressed in this strand.

Identifies Strand/Domain

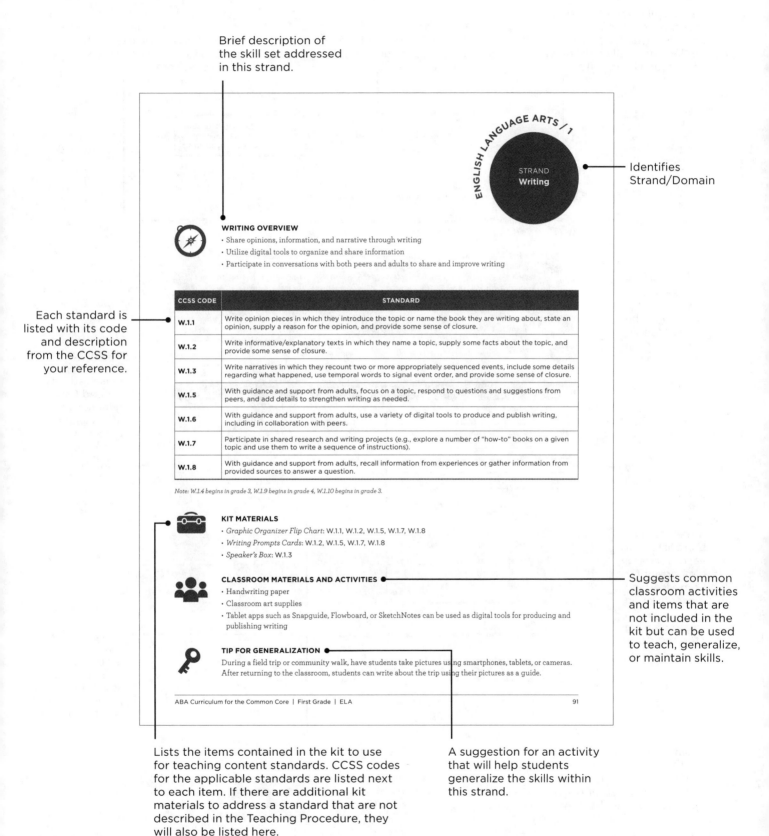

ENGLISH LANGUAGE ARTS / 1

STRAND
Writing

WRITING OVERVIEW
- Share opinions, information, and narrative through writing
- Utilize digital tools to organize and share information
- Participate in conversations with both peers and adults to share and improve writing

Each standard is listed with its code and description from the CCSS for your reference.

CCSS CODE	STANDARD
W.1.1	Write opinion pieces in which they introduce the topic or name the book they are writing about, state an opinion, supply a reason for the opinion, and provide some sense of closure.
W.1.2	Write informative/explanatory texts in which they name a topic, supply some facts about the topic, and provide some sense of closure.
W.1.3	Write narratives in which they recount two or more appropriately sequenced events, include some details regarding what happened, use temporal words to signal event order, and provide some sense of closure.
W.1.5	With guidance and support from adults, focus on a topic, respond to questions and suggestions from peers, and add details to strengthen writing as needed.
W.1.6	With guidance and support from adults, use a variety of digital tools to produce and publish writing, including in collaboration with peers.
W.1.7	Participate in shared research and writing projects (e.g., explore a number of "how-to" books on a given topic and use them to write a sequence of instructions).
W.1.8	With guidance and support from adults, recall information from experiences or gather information from provided sources to answer a question.

Note: W.1.4 begins in grade 3, W.1.9 begins in grade 4, W.1.10 begins in grade 3.

KIT MATERIALS
- *Graphic Organizer Flip Chart*: W.1.1, W.1.2, W.1.5, W.1.7, W.1.8
- *Writing Prompts Cards*: W.1.2, W.1.5, W.1.7, W.1.8
- *Speaker's Box*: W.1.3

CLASSROOM MATERIALS AND ACTIVITIES
- Handwriting paper
- Classroom art supplies
- Tablet apps such as Snapguide, Flowboard, or SketchNotes can be used as digital tools for producing and publishing writing

Suggests common classroom activities and items that are not included in the kit but can be used to teach, generalize, or maintain skills.

TIP FOR GENERALIZATION
During a field trip or community walk, have students take pictures using smartphones, tablets, or cameras. After returning to the classroom, students can write about the trip using their pictures as a guide.

ABA Curriculum for the Common Core | First Grade | ELA   91

Lists the items contained in the kit to use for teaching content standards. CCSS codes for the applicable standards are listed next to each item. If there are additional kit materials to address a standard that are not described in the Teaching Procedure, they will also be listed here.

A suggestion for an activity that will help students generalize the skills within this strand.

Standard Reference Page

These sheets can be reproduced for each student to track progress on each standard. Supplemental daily data sheets can be found in Appendix C.

This header notes the Strand, Cluster, and the Standards included for easy reference.

The kit materials described in the Teaching Procedure are marked in bold. Other materials included in the kit that can be used to teach, generalize or maintain the skill are also listed here.

CCSS Standard addressed by this program.

The Teaching Procedure presents one suggestion for how to use the included kit materials to teach the standard.

The discriminative stimulus (or Sd) is what you say or do to evoke a response. Two to three potential Sds are listed for each standard. It is important for long-term learning and generalization to vary the Sd instead of using the same one each time.

Enter the date the target was introduced, mastered, and probed for generalization, along with the initials of the instructor.

Indicates the Kindergarten CCSS Standard(s) to drill down to if student is not able to meet the First Grade target.

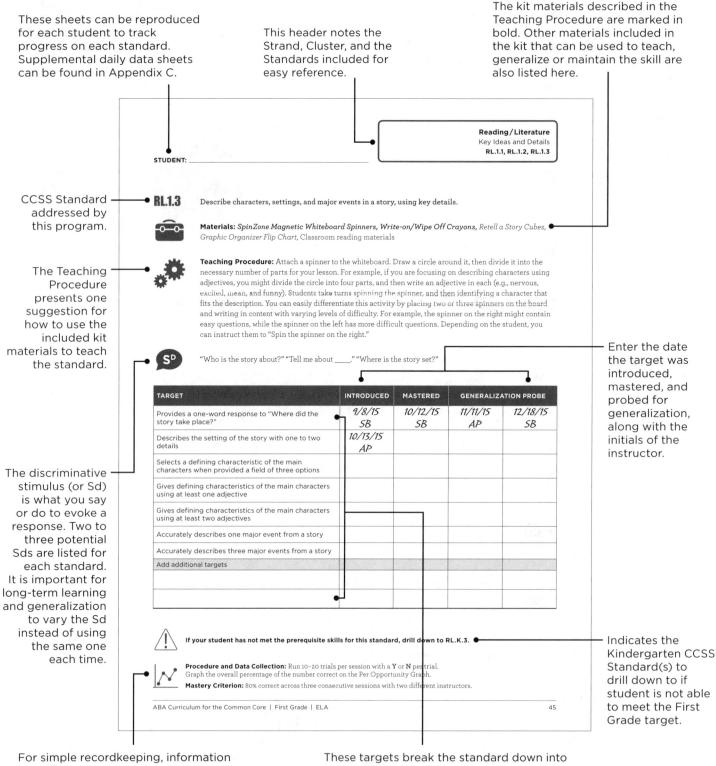

Reading/Literature
Key Ideas and Details
RL.1.1, RL.1.2, RL.1.3

STUDENT: _____

RL.1.3   Describe characters, settings, and major events in a story, using key details.

Materials: *SpinZone Magnetic Whiteboard Spinners, Write-on/Wipe Off Crayons,* Retell a Story Cubes, *Graphic Organizer Flip Chart,* Classroom reading materials

Teaching Procedure: Attach a spinner to the whiteboard. Draw a circle around it, then divide it into the necessary number of parts for your lesson. For example, if you are focusing on describing characters using adjectives, you might divide the circle into four parts, and then write an adjective in each (e.g., nervous, excited, mean, and funny). Students take turns spinning the spinner, and then identifying a character that fits the description. You can easily differentiate this activity by placing two or three spinners on the board and writing in content with varying levels of difficulty. For example, the spinner on the right might contain easy questions, while the spinner on the left has more difficult questions. Depending on the student, you can instruct them to "Spin the spinner on the right."

S^D   "Who is the story about?" "Tell me about _____." "Where is the story set?"

TARGET	INTRODUCED	MASTERED	GENERALIZATION PROBE	
Provides a one-word response to "Where did the story take place?"	9/8/15 SB	10/12/15 SB	11/11/15 AP	12/18/15 SB
Describes the setting of the story with one to two details	10/13/15 AP			
Selects a defining characteristic of the main characters when provided a field of three options				
Gives defining characteristics of the main characters using at least one adjective				
Gives defining characteristics of the main characters using at least two adjectives				
Accurately describes one major event from a story				
Accurately describes three major events from a story				
Add additional targets				

⚠   If your student has not met the prerequisite skills for this standard, drill down to RL.K.3.

📈   **Procedure and Data Collection:** Run 10–20 trials per session with a **Y** or **N** per trial. Graph the overall percentage of the number correct on the Per Opportunity Graph.
Mastery Criterion: 80% correct across three consecutive sessions with two different instructors.

For simple recordkeeping, information about how many trials to run during a session, as well as criteria that students must meet in order for the skill to be mastered are listed here. All data can be collected on forms provided in Appendix C.

These targets break the standard down into prerequisite steps and skills that your student should master in order to meet the standard. You may need to add additional prerequisite skills to meet the unique needs of an individual student so there are blank boxes for you to add your own targets.

The Big Picture

Our goal with this kit is to supply you with tools to make the Common Core State Standards for ELA and Math accessible to students with special needs by breaking down each standard into teachable steps and providing an ABA framework to increase student success. The materials and information provided in this kit also serve to better prepare you to utilize ABA with all of your students. The evidence-based strategies described here have been proven to have significant impacts on students with autism, as well as a range of other disabilities such as ADHD and Down Syndrome. We hope this kit will allow you to prepare individualized lessons aligned with Common Core State Standards, track student progress effectively, and embrace creativity in your teaching to meet the everyday challenges presented in your classroom.

We wish you the best of luck and success.

LITERATURE OVERVIEW

- Participate in conversations about both familiar and novel texts
- Identify the main idea and supporting details of a text
- Compare and contrast characters, stories, and types of texts

CCSS CODE	STANDARD
RL.1.1	Ask and answer questions about key details in a text.
RL.1.2	Retell stories, including key details, and demonstrate understanding of their central message or lesson.
RL.1.3	Describe characters, settings, and major events in a story, using key details.
RL.1.4	Identify words and phrases in stories or poems that suggest feelings or appeal to the senses.
RL.1.5	Explain major differences between books that tell stories and books that give information, drawing on a wide reading of a range of text types.
RL.1.6	Identify who is telling the story at various points in a text.
RL.1.7	Use illustrations and details in a story to describe its characters, setting, or events.
RL.1.9	Compare and contrast the adventures and experiences of characters in stories.
RL.1.10	With prompting and support, read prose and poetry of appropriate complexity for grade 1.

Note: RL.1.8 not applicable to Literature.

KIT MATERIALS

- *Parts of a Story Thumball*: RL.1.1
- *Tell the Tale Thumball*: RL.1.2, RL.1.9
- *Retell A Story Cubes*: RL.1.2, RL.1.3
- *Graphic Organizer Flip Chart*: RL.1.2, RL.1.3, RL.1.4, RL.1.5, RL.1.9
- *SpinZone Magnetic Whiteboard Spinners*: RL.1.3, RL.1.6, RL.1.9
- *Write-on/Wipe-off Crayons*: RL.1.3
- *Speaker's Box*: RL.1.7

(continued)

CLASSROOM MATERIALS AND ACTIVITIES

- Classroom reading materials
- Puppets, figurines, or other characters
- Felt cut-outs for retelling familiar stories
- Episodes of favorite TV shows, cartoons, or YouTube videos

TIP FOR GENERALIZATION

Utilize magazines created for children such as *National Geographic for Kids* or *Disney Junior* to find highly motivating materials for your students to practice these standards.

STUDENT: _____

RL.1.1   Ask and answer questions about key details in a text.

Materials: *Parts of a Story Thumball*, Classroom reading materials

Teaching Procedure: Read a story with the class. After the story is complete, toss the *Parts of a Story Thumball* to different students. When the student catches it, he or she must answer the question under his/her thumb. If your students struggle with catching the ball, you can modify the activity by placing color cards that correspond to the colors on the ball on the table. The student chooses a color card, then finds and reads the question on the matching color on the ball.

"Who is the story about?" "Tell me what happened after ___." "What happened in the story?"

TARGET	INTRODUCED	MASTERED	GENERALIZATION PROBE	
Responds to "who," "what," and "where" questions about the text				
When asked, identifies both the problem and the solution in the story				
Responds to "when" questions about the text				
Responds to "why" questions about the text				
Asks "who" questions about the text				
Asks "where" questions about the text				
Asks "what" questions about the text				
Add additional targets				

If your student has not met the prerequisite skills for this standard, drill down to RL.K.1.

Procedure and Data Collection: Run 10–20 trials per session with a **Y** or **N** per trial. Graph the overall percentage of the number correct on the Per Opportunity Graph.

Mastery Criterion: 80% correct across three consecutive sessions with two different instructors.

STUDENT: _____

RL.1.2   Retell stories, including key details, and demonstrate understanding of their central message or lesson.

Materials: *Graphic Organizer Flip Chart*, *Tell the Tale Thumball*, *Retell a Story Cubes*, Classroom reading materials

Teaching Procedure: Use the "Story Map" page in the *Graphic Organizer Flip Chart Activity Book*, making sure you have a copy for each student. Guide students through retelling the story using the Map. If your lesson focuses on a central message from the story, you may consider using the "Web" from the *Graphic Organizer Flip Chart*. Write the central message in the center circle, then help students generate examples of the message from the text to place in the outer circles.

"What is this story mainly about?" "Can you tell me the story in your own words?"

TARGET	INTRODUCED	MASTERED	GENERALIZATION PROBE	
Completes fill-ins for a 5–10 sentence story (e.g., "This story is about a girl named ___.")				
Retells a 5–10 sentence story with prompting				
Retells a 5–10 sentence story in sequence				
Retells a 10–15 sentence story in sequence				
Identifies what a story is mainly about in one sentence				
Add additional targets				

If your student has not met the prerequisite skills for this standard, drill down to RL.K.2.

Procedure and Data Collection: Run 10–20 trials per session with a **Y** or **N** per trial. Graph the overall percentage of the number correct on the Per Opportunity Graph.

Mastery Criterion: 80% correct across three consecutive sessions with two different instructors.

STUDENT: _____

RL.1.3 Describe characters, settings, and major events in a story, using key details.

Materials: *SpinZone Magnetic Whiteboard Spinners, Write-on/Wipe Off Crayons,* Retell a Story Cubes, *Graphic Organizer Flip Chart,* Classroom reading materials

Teaching Procedure: Attach a spinner to the whiteboard. Draw a circle around it, then divide it into the necessary number of parts for your lesson. For example, if you are focusing on describing characters using adjectives, you might divide the circle into four parts, and then write an adjective in each (e.g., nervous, excited, mean, and funny). Students take turns spinning the spinner, and then identifying a character that fits the description. You can easily differentiate this activity by placing two or three spinners on the board and writing in content with varying levels of difficulty. For example, the spinner on the right might contain easy questions, while the spinner on the left has more difficult questions. Depending on the student, you can instruct them to "Spin the spinner on the right."

"Who is the story about?" "Tell me about _____." "Where is the story set?"

TARGET	INTRODUCED	MASTERED	GENERALIZATION PROBE
Provides a one-word response to "Where did the story take place?"			
Describes the setting of the story with one to two details			
Selects a defining characteristic of the main characters when provided a field of three options			
Gives defining characteristics of the main characters using at least one adjective			
Gives defining characteristics of the main characters using at least two adjectives			
Accurately describes one major event from a story			
Accurately describes three major events from a story			
Add additional targets			

If your student has not met the prerequisite skills for this standard, drill down to RL.K.3.

Procedure and Data Collection: Run 10–20 trials per session with a **Y** or **N** per trial. Graph the overall percentage of the number correct on the Per Opportunity Graph.

Mastery Criterion: 80% correct across three consecutive sessions with two different instructors.

STUDENT: _____

RL.1.4 Identify words and phrases in stories or poems that suggest feelings or appeal to the senses.

Materials: *Graphic Organizer Flip Chart*, Classroom reading materials

Teaching Procedure: Use the "Web" page in the *Graphic Organizer Flip Chart Activity Book*, making sure you have a copy for each student. Guide students through a discussion to identify feelings. For example, if a character is feeling sad, place the word "sad" in the center circle, and then have students refer to the text to find words and phrases that suggest sadness, such as "he began to cry" or "his shoulders slumped." If the text you are reading relates more to words that appeal to the senses, you may find the "Observation" page of the *Graphic Organizer Flip Chart* more beneficial.

"How did ___ feel when ___?" "How do you know she/he felt that way?" "Why did she/he feel that way?"

TARGET	INTRODUCED	MASTERED	GENERALIZATION PROBE	
Identifies clearly defined emotion in the text (e.g., the text states, "He was sad.")				
Identifies emotions that are alluded to in the text (e.g., the text states, "He began to cry.")				
States what clues in the text showed emotion				
Explains why a character might feel a certain way (saying he was sad because he was crying is incorrect, but saying he was sad because the girl took his toy away is correct.)				
Identifies words and phrases from the text that appeal to the senses (such as sights, sounds, etc.) for at least two senses				
Identifies words and phrases from the text that appeal to the senses (such as sights, sounds, etc.) for all five senses				
Identifies how a person might feel based on words and phrases appealing to the senses (such as how a person feels when they smell cookies or hear a fire alarm)				
Add additional target				

If your student has not met the prerequisite skills for this standard, drill down to RL.K.4.

Procedure and Data Collection: Run 10–20 trials per session with a **Y** or **N** per trial.
Graph the overall percentage of the number correct on the Per Opportunity Graph.

Mastery Criterion: 80% correct across three consecutive sessions with two different instructors.

STUDENT: _____

RL.1.5 Explain major differences between books that tell stories and books that give information, drawing on a wide reading of a range of text types.

Materials: *Graphic Organizer Flip Chart*, Classroom reading materials

Teaching Procedure: Use the "Venn Diagram" page of the *Graphic Organizer Flip Chart*. Ask questions to help your students compare and contrast two stories or books. If your students struggle with reading or managing multiple pieces of information, you may want to use pictures on the Venn Diagram. For example, if you are comparing a book about whales to a book about dolphins, place a picture of the whale above the left-hand circle of the diagram, and a picture of a dolphin above the right-hand circle of the diagram.

"How are these two books different?" "Which book is pretend?" "Name a book that gives information."

TARGET	INTRODUCED	MASTERED	GENERALIZATION PROBE	
When presented with a field of three familiar books, identifies which books tell stories and which books give information				
Describes a book that tells stories as "not real," "fiction," or "pretend"				
Describes a book that gives information as "real," "nonfiction," or "helpful"				
Provides three examples of books that tell stories and three examples of books that give information				
Add additional targets				

If your student has not met the prerequisite skills for this standard, drill down to RL.K.5.

Procedure and Data Collection: Run 10–20 trials per session with a **Y** or **N** per trial. Graph the overall percentage of the number correct on the Per Opportunity Graph.

Mastery Criterion: 80% correct across three consecutive sessions with two different instructors.

RL.1.6

Identify who is telling the story at various points in a text.

Materials: *SpinZone Magnetic Whiteboard Spinners,* Classroom reading materials such as "The Rainbow Fish" by Marcus Pfister or "Moondance" by Frank Asch

Teaching Procedure: Attach a spinner to the whiteboard. Draw a circle around it, and then divide it into the necessary number of parts for your lesson. For example, if you are focusing on three characters from the story, divide the circle into three parts, then write a character's name in each section. Students take turns spinning the spinner, saying the character's name, and then giving an example of what that character said in the story. You can easily differentiate this activity by placing two or three spinners on the board and writing in content with varying levels of difficulty. For example, the spinner on the right might contain easy questions, while the spinner on the left has more difficult questions. Depending on the student, you can instruct them to "Spin the spinner on the right."

S^D "Who is the narrator?" "Who is telling us the story?" "Can you tell me who is talking now?"

TARGET	INTRODUCED	MASTERED	GENERALIZATION PROBE	
Points to the narrator pictured on the page for a least three different texts				
Points to the character speaking within a story for at least three different texts				
Identifies who the narrator was after completing the story for at least three different texts				
Add additional targets				

If your student has not met the prerequisite skills for this standard, drill down to RL.K.6.

Procedure and Data Collection: Run 10–20 trials per session with a **Y** or **N** per trial. Graph the overall percentage of the number correct on the Per Opportunity Graph.

Mastery Criterion: 80% correct across three consecutive sessions with two different instructors.

STUDENT: _____

 RL.1.7 Use illustrations and details in a story to describe its characters, setting, or events.

 Materials: *Speaker's Box,* Classroom reading materials

 Teaching Procedure: Remove all cards except for the black cards from the *Speaker's Box*. Have students take turns taking pictures out of the box, describing what is happening, and sharing what could happen next. You can modify the activity by adding your own pictures based on your students' current skill levels or reading activities you've completed in class. You can also ask such questions during or immediately after a reading activity by pointing to images or characters in different illustrations.

 "Show me ___." "Who is in this picture?" "What is happening in this picture?"

TARGET	INTRODUCED	MASTERED	GENERALIZATION PROBE	
Points to characters in an illustration when the teacher names them for up to three characters				
Points to characters in an illustration when the teacher names them for up to five characters in three different books				
Points to characters in an illustration when the teacher names them in novel stories and books				
Points to actions in an illustration when the teacher names them for up to three actions				
Points to actions in an illustration when the teacher names them for up to five actions				
Points to actions in an illustration when the teacher names them in novel stories and books				
Looks at an illustration and names the characters pictured without prompts from the teacher for up to three books				
Looks at an illustration and names the setting without prompts from the teacher (i.e., names that the story takes place "on the playground")				
Add additional target				

 If your student has not met the prerequisite skills for this standard, drill down to RL.K.7.

 Procedure and Data Collection: Run 10-20 trials per session with a **Y** or **N** per trial. Graph the overall percentage of the number correct on the Per Opportunity Graph.

Mastery Criterion: 80% correct across three consecutive sessions with two different instructors.

RL.1.9

Compare and contrast the adventures and experiences of characters in stories.

Materials: *Graphic Organizer Flip Chart*, Classroom reading materials

Teaching Procedure: Use the "Venn Diagram" page of the *Graphic Organizer Flip Chart*. Ask questions to help your students compare and contrast two characters. If your students struggle with reading or managing multiple pieces of information, you may want to use pictures on the Venn Diagram. For example, place one character's picture over one circle and the other character's picture over the other circle. You can also use pictures for other elements of the story. If both characters had an adventure on a river, you can place a picture of the river in the space where the circles overlap.

"How is ___'s problem similar to ___'s problem?" "What is different about the story of ___ and the story of ___?" "Tell me how they are similar."

TARGET	INTRODUCED	MASTERED	GENERALIZATION PROBE	
When presented with choices, tells which characters from familiar stories had similar adventures and experiences				
When presented with choices, tells which characters from familiar stories had different adventures and experiences				
Compares and contrasts adventures and experiences of two characters from familiar texts				
Compares and contrasts the character's experiences in a novel text to that of a previously read text				
Add additional targets				

If your student has not met the prerequisite skills for this standard, drill down to RL.K.9.

Procedure and Data Collection: Run 10–20 trials per session with a **Y** or **N** per trial. Graph the overall percentage of the number correct on the Per Opportunity Graph.

Mastery Criterion: 80% correct across three consecutive sessions with two different instructors.

STUDENT: _____

RL.1.10 With prompting and support, read prose and poetry of appropriate complexity for grade 1.

Materials: Storybook or other reading materials from classroom

Teaching Procedure: Create a clear routine for independent reading activities. This may include audio or visual cues. Support interest in reading by helping each student select materials that are at an appropriate reading level and are highly motivating for that individual.

"Let's read." "Can you read here?"

TARGET	INTRODUCED	MASTERED	GENERALIZATION PROBE	
With prompting and support, reads 1–3 sentences				
With prompting and support, reads a page of grade 1 text				
With prompting and support, reads a grade 1 poem				
Add additional targets				

If your student has not met the prerequisite skills for this standard, drill down to RL.K.10.

Procedure and Data Collection: Run 10–20 trials per session with a **Y** or **N** per trial.
Graph the overall percentage of the number correct on the Per Opportunity Graph.

Mastery Criterion: 80% correct across three consecutive sessions with two different instructors.

INFORMATIONAL TEXT OVERVIEW

- Participate in meaningful conversation about informational texts
- Identify the main idea, supporting detail, and text features of an informational text
- Compare and contrast texts on the same subject as well as individuals, events, and ideas within a text

CCSS CODE	STANDARD
RI.1.1	Ask and answer questions about key details in a text.
RI.1.2	Identify the main topic and retell key details of a text.
RI.1.3	Describe the connection between two individuals, events, ideas, or pieces of information in a text.
RI.1.4	Ask and answer questions to help determine or clarify the meaning of words and phrases in a text.
RI.1.5	Know and use various text features (e.g., headings, tables of contents, glossaries, electronic menus, icons) to locate key facts or information in a text.
RI.1.6	Distinguish between information provided by pictures or other illustrations and information provided by the words in a text.
RI.1.7	Use the illustrations and details in a text to describe its key ideas.
RI.1.8	Identify the reasons an author gives to support points in a text.
RI.1.9	Identify basic similarities in and differences between two texts on the same topic (e.g., in illustrations, descriptions, or procedures).
RI.1.10	With prompting and support, read informational texts appropriately complex for grade 1.

KIT MATERIALS

- *Graphic Organizer Flip Chart*: RI.1.1, RI.1.2, RI.1.3, RI.1.8, RI.1.9
- *Parts of a Story Thumball*: RI.1.1, RI.1.2
- *SpinZone Magnetic Whiteboard Spinners*: RI.1.4
- *Write-on/Wipe-off Crayons*: RI.1.4
- *Drawing Conclusions Reading Comprehension Cards*: RI.1.6, RI.1.7

CLASSROOM MATERIALS AND ACTIVITIES

- Classroom books
- Newspapers
- Age-appropriate publications such as *National Geographic for Kids* or *Kids Discover for Young Readers*

(continued)

TIP FOR GENERALIZATION

Create an information scavenger hunt. Students can work individually or in teams to search through teacher-selected informational texts and write down or verbally share which texts might provide information about specific topics. They should be able to support their responses by indicating headings, illustrations, and other text features. For example, three books about bears are available. One item on the scavenger hunt might be "Where do bears live?" The student could support their answer by showing the heading "habitat" in one of the books.

STUDENT: _____

RI.1.1 Ask and answer questions about key details in a text.

Materials: *Graphic Organizer Flip Chart*, *Parts of a Story Thumball,* Classroom reading materials

Teaching Procedure: Use the "5 W's" page in the *Graphic Organizer Flip Chart Activity Book,* making sure you have enough copies for each student. Guide students through the process of responding to questions about the text and filling in the graphic organizer. It may be beneficial to utilize visual cues. For some learners, it may be appropriate to use the "5 W's" graphic organizer as a visual prompt for generating questions about the text.

"What happened in this story?" "Where does this story take place?" "Can you come up with a 'where' question about the text?"

TARGET	INTRODUCED	MASTERED	GENERALIZATION PROBE	
Responds to "who," "what," and "where" questions about the text				
Responds to a random rotation of all five wh- questions about the text				
Responds with one fact to "What did you learn from the text?"				
Responds with two to three facts to "What did you learn from the text?"				
With prompts, generates one question about a text for three or more texts				
Independently generates one question about a text for three or more texts				
With prompts, generates two to three questions about a text for three or more texts				
Independently generates two to three questions about a text for three or more texts				
Add additional target				

If your student has not met the prerequisite skills for this standard, drill down to RI.K.1.

Procedure and Data Collection: Run 10–20 trials per session with a **Y** or **N** per trial. Graph the overall percentage of the number correct on the Per Opportunity Graph.

Mastery Criterion: 80% correct across three consecutive sessions with two different instructors.

STUDENT: _____

RI.1.2   Identify the main topic and retell key details of a text.

Materials: *Parts of a Story Thumball, Graphic Organizer Flip Chart,* Informational text

Teaching Procedure: Have an informational text available for students to reference after reading is complete. Toss the *Parts of a Story Thumball* to different students. When the student catches it, he or she must answer the question under his/her thumb. If your students struggle with catching the ball, you can modify the activity by placing color cards that correspond to the colors on the ball on the table. The student chooses a color card, then finds and reads the question on the matching color on the ball.

"What is this story mostly about?" "How do you know the author feels this way?" "What is one thing you learned?"

TARGET	INTRODUCED	MASTERED	GENERALIZATION PROBE
Responds to "What is this mostly about?"			
When provided with the main idea, retells one key detail from the text			
When provided with the main idea, retells three key details from the text			
Retells information from the text including the main idea and key details			
Add additional targets			

   If your student has not met the prerequisite skills for this standard, drill down to RI.K.2.

   Procedure and Data Collection: Run 10–20 trials per session with a **Y** or **N** per trial. Graph the overall percentage of the number correct on the Per Opportunity Graph.

Mastery Criterion: 80% correct across three consecutive sessions with two different instructors.

STUDENT: _____

RI.1.3 Describe the connection between two individuals, events, ideas, or pieces of information in a text.

Materials: *Graphic Organizer Flip Chart,* Classroom reading materials

Teaching Procedure: Use the "Venn Diagram" page of the *Graphic Organizer Flip Chart*. Ask questions to help your students compare and contrast two characters. If your students struggle with reading or managing multiple pieces of information, you may want to use pictures on the Venn diagram. For example, place one character's picture over one circle and the other character's picture over the other circle. You can also use pictures for other elements of the story. If both characters had an adventure on a river, you can place a picture of the river in the space where the circles overlap.

S^D "What do they have in common?" "What idea do both stories talk about?"

TARGET	INTRODUCED	MASTERED	GENERALIZATION PROBE	
Tells how two individuals from a text are connected to one another				
Tells how two individuals from a text are connected for a novel text				
Tells how two events from a text are connected for three different texts				
Tells how two events from a text are connected for a novel text				
Tells how two pieces of information from a text are connected for three different texts				
Tells how two pieces of information are connected for a novel text				
Tells how two ideas from a text are connected for three different texts				
Tells how two ideas from a text are connected for a novel text				
Add additional target				

 If your student has not met the prerequisite skills for this standard, drill down to RI.K.3.

 Procedure and Data Collection: Run 10-20 trials per session with a **Y** or **N** per trial. Graph the overall percentage of the number correct on the Per Opportunity Graph.

Mastery Criterion: 80% correct across three consecutive sessions with two different instructors.

STUDENT: _____

RI.1.4   Ask and answer questions to help determine or clarify the meaning of words and phrases in a text.

Materials: *SpinZone Magnetic Whiteboard Spinners, Write-on/Wipe-off Crayons*

Teaching Procedure: Attach a spinner to the whiteboard. Draw a circle around it, and then divide it into the necessary number of parts for your lesson. For example, if you are focusing on six particular vocabulary words, divide the circle into six parts, and then write a vocabulary word in each section. Students take turns spinning the spinner and then reading a sentence or short passage that contains that word. Guide the student through the process of using context clues to determine the meaning of the word. You can easily differentiate this activity by placing two or three spinners on the board and writing in content with varying levels of difficulty. For example, the spinner on the right might contain easy questions, while the spinner on the left has more difficult questions. Depending on the student, you can instruct them to "Spin the spinner on the right."

S^D   "I wonder what that means." Pause to allow time for the learner to ask about the meaning of the word, provide a gestural prompt (such as a point) if necessary. "Where can we look for clues to the meaning of that word?"

TARGET	INTRODUCED	MASTERED	GENERALIZATION PROBE	
When teacher points to a word and asks, "Hmmm, I wonder what this means," student responds, "I don't know" or responds with definition				
When teacher provides gestural prompt (pointing) or conversational prompt ("Hmmm") student asks, "What does that word mean?"				
Independently asks what an unknown word means				
Looks at other words in the sentence for context clues				
Makes appropriate guesses about the meaning of an unknown word based on context clues				
Add additional targets				

 If your student has not met the prerequisite skills for this standard, drill down to RI.K.4.

 Procedure and Data Collection: Run 10–20 trials per session with a **Y** or **N** per trial. Graph the overall percentage of the number correct on the Per Opportunity Graph.

Mastery Criterion: 80% correct across three consecutive sessions with two different instructors.

STUDENT: _____

RI.1.5 Know and use various text features (e.g., headings, tables of contents, glossaries, electronic menus, icons) to locate key facts or information in a text.

Materials: Classroom reading materials

Teaching Procedure: Bring a selection of informational texts to the table. The examples you pick should all have chapters and/or headings. Open up a book, point to the heading and choose a student to read it aloud. Then, ask students to share what you might learn about in that section of the text. You can also point out two different headings and ask students which one is more likely to contain information about particular topic.

"Where is the heading?" "Where might we find information about _____?" "Can you find the meaning of the word _____?"

TARGET	INTRODUCED	MASTERED	GENERALIZATION PROBE	
Points to a heading when named for at least three texts				
Points to the table of contents when named for at least three texts				
Points to the glossary when named for at least three texts				
Locates electronic menus when named for at least three electronic texts				
Locates icons when named for at least three electronic texts				
Uses headings to respond to questions for at least three texts				
Uses the table of contents to respond to questions for at least three texts				
Uses the glossary to respond to questions for at least three texts				
Uses electronic menus to respond to questions for at least three electronic texts				
Uses icons to respond to questions for at least three electronic texts				
Add additional target				

 If your student has not met the prerequisite skills for this standard, drill down to RI.K.5.

 Procedure and Data Collection: Run 10–20 trials per session with a **Y** or **N** per trial. Graph the overall percentage of the number correct on the Per Opportunity Graph.

Mastery Criterion: 80% correct across three consecutive sessions with two different instructors.

RI.1.6 Distinguish between information provided by pictures or other illustrations and information provided by the words in a text.

Materials: *Drawing Conclusions Reading Comprehension Cards*

Teaching Procedure: Hold up one story card from the *Drawing Conclusions* deck. Ask students questions about the picture they see. Some of the questions you ask should be easy to answer based on the picture, while others will require reading the text. If the students can't answer a question, ask them where they think they might find the answer. Then read the story with students and answer the question on the card. After answering the question, have students tell you what they did to figure out the correct answer.

"What do we know about the story from the picture?" "Did you figure out the answer by looking at the picture or reading the text?"

TARGET	INTRODUCED	MASTERED	GENERALIZATION PROBE	
When asked wh- questions, refers to an illustration to respond correctly for at least three texts				
When asked wh- questions, refers to an illustration to respond correctly for at least five texts				
When asked wh- questions, refers to an illustration to respond correctly for a novel text				
When asked wh- questions, refers to words in the text to respond correctly for at least three texts				
When asked wh- questions, refers to words in the text to respond correctly for at least five texts				
When asked wh- questions, refers to words in the text to respond correctly for a novel text				
When asked wh- questions, identifies if the answer is found in an illustration or words in the text for three texts				
When asked wh- questions, identifies if the answer is found in an illustration or words in the text for five texts				
When asked wh- questions, identifies if the answer is found in an illustration or words in the text for a novel text				
When asked to identify a caption, points to a caption in the text for three texts				

(continued)

STUDENT: _____

(RI.1.6 page 2)

When asked to identify a caption, points to a caption in the text for five texts				
When asked to identify a caption, points to a caption in the text for a novel text				
States the definition for a caption when asked				
Add additional targets				

 If your student has not met the prerequisite skills for this standard, drill down to RI.K.6.

 Procedure and Data Collection: Run 10-20 trials per session with a **Y** or **N** per trial. Graph the overall percentage of the number correct on the Per Opportunity Graph.

Mastery Criterion: 80% correct across three consecutive sessions with two different instructors.

STUDENT: _____

RI.1.7   Use the illustrations and details in a text to describe its key ideas.

Materials: *Drawing Conclusions Reading Comprehension Cards*

Teaching Procedure: Hold up one story card from the *Drawing Conclusions* deck. Have students look at the picture, and then read the story aloud. Ask the students what the story is about. As students respond, require them to provide specific examples from the illustrations and text to support their statements. When using other informational texts, "illustration" may refer to graphs, charts, or other depictions of information that the students must be able to understand and describe.

"What information does this illustration provide?" "How does the illustration tell us about the ___?" "Can you look at the text and tell me more about ___?" "Where did you find that information?"

TARGET	INTRODUCED	MASTERED	GENERALIZATION PROBE	
Identifies key idea of text for three texts				
Identifies key idea of text for five texts				
Identifies key idea of text for a novel text				
References an illustration to describe key idea for three texts				
References an illustration to describe key idea for five texts				
References an illustration to describe key idea for a novel text				
References details in a text to describe key idea for three texts				
References details in a text to describe key idea for five texts				
References details in a text to describe key idea for a novel text				
Add additional targets				

   If your student has not met the prerequisite skills for this standard, drill down to RI.K.7.

   Procedure and Data Collection: Run 10–20 trials per session with a **Y** or **N** per trial. Graph the overall percentage of the number correct on the Per Opportunity Graph.

Mastery Criterion: 80% correct across three consecutive sessions with two different instructors.

STUDENT: _____

RI.1.8   Identify the reasons an author gives to support points in a text.

Materials: *Graphic Organizer Flip Chart,* Classroom reading materials

Teaching Procedure: Introduce the "Web" or "Star" graphics from the *Graphic Organizer Flip Chart.* Write the author's point in the center space. Provide prompting and support to help students identify reasons the author gives in the text to support the point.

"What does the author say about ___?" "Why does the author think ___?" "Can you share a supporting detail?"

TARGET	INTRODUCED	MASTERED	GENERALIZATION PROBE
With prompting and support, identifies one supporting point from the text			
With prompting and support, identifies two to three supporting points from the text			
Independently identifies one supporting point from the text			
Independently identifies two to three supporting points from the text			
Add additional targets			

If your student has not met the prerequisite skills for this standard, drill down to RI.K.8.

Procedure and Data Collection: Run 10–20 trials per session with a **Y** or **N** per trial. Graph the overall percentage of the number correct on the Per Opportunity Graph.

Mastery Criterion: 80% correct across three consecutive sessions with two different instructors.

STUDENT: _____

RI.1.9 Identify basic similarities in and differences between two texts on the same topic (e.g., in illustrations, descriptions, or procedures).

Materials: *Graphic Organizer Flip Chart,* Classroom reading materials

Teaching Procedure: Use the "Venn Diagram" page of the *Graphic Organizer Flip Chart.* Ask questions to help your students compare and contrast two stories or books. If your students struggle with reading or managing multiple pieces of information, you may want to use pictures on the Venn diagram. For example, if you are comparing two books about airplanes, place images related to one book over the left-hand circle of the diagram, and images related to the other book above the right-hand circle of the diagram.

"How are the illustrations in this book different from the illustrations in the other book?" "How are they the same?" "What did this author say about ___?"

TARGET	INTRODUCED	MASTERED	GENERALIZATION PROBE	
With prompting and support, identifies one similarity between two texts on the same topic				
With prompting and support, identifies at least three similarities between two texts on the same topic				
Independently identifies one similarity between two texts on the same topic				
Independently identifies at least three similarities between two texts on the same topic				
With prompting and support, identifies one difference between two texts on the same topic				
With prompting and support, identifies at least three differences between two texts on the same topic				
Independently identifies one difference between two texts on the same topic				
Independently identifies at least three differences between two texts on the same topic				
Add additional target				

⚠️ **If your student has not met the prerequisite skills for this standard, drill down to RI.K.9.**

Procedure and Data Collection: Run 10–20 trials per session with a **Y** or **N** per trial. Graph the overall percentage of the number correct on the Per Opportunity Graph.

Mastery Criterion: 80% correct across three consecutive sessions with two different instructors.

STUDENT: _____

RI.1.10   With prompting and support, read informational texts appropriately complex for grade 1.

Materials: Classroom reading materials

Teaching Procedure: Create a clear routine for independent reading activities. This may include audio or visual cues. Support student interest in reading by helping each student select materials that are at an appropriate reading level and are highly motivating for that individual.

"Let's read." "Can you read here?"

TARGET	INTRODUCED	MASTERED	GENERALIZATION PROBE	
With prompting and support, reads one to three sentences of an informational text				
With prompting and support, reads a page of a grade 1 informational text				
With prompting and support, selects appropriately complex texts when presented with a field of three texts				
With prompting and support, selects appropriately complex texts when presented with a field of five texts				
With prompting and support, selects appropriately complex texts when presented with a section of books in the library				
Add additional targets				

If your student has not met the prerequisite skills for this standard, drill down to RI.K.10.

Procedure and Data Collection: Run 10–20 trials per session with a **Y** or **N** per trial. Graph the overall percentage of the number correct on the Per Opportunity Graph.

Mastery Criterion: 80% correct across three consecutive sessions with two different instructors.

FOUNDATIONAL SKILLS OVERVIEW
· Decode one- and two-syllable words
· Demonstrate understanding of common spelling conventions
· Recognize common features of a sentence
· Read first-grade level texts with accuracy and fluency

CCSS CODE	STANDARD
RF.1.1	Demonstrate understanding of the organization and basic features of print.
RF.1.1.a	Recognize the distinguishing features of a sentence (e.g., first word, capitalization, ending punctuation).
RF.1.2	Demonstrate understanding of spoken words, syllables, and sounds (phonemes).
RF.1.2.a	Distinguish long from short vowel sounds in spoken single-syllable words.
RF.1.2.b	Orally produce single-syllable words by blending sounds (phonemes), including consonant blends.
RF.1.2.c	Isolate and pronounce initial, medial vowel, and final sounds (phonemes) in spoken single-syllable words.
RF.1.2.d	Segment spoken single-syllable words into their complete sequence of individual sounds (phonemes).
RF.1.3	Know and apply grade-level phonics and word analysis skills in decoding words.
RF.1.3.a	Know the spelling-sound correspondences for common consonant digraphs.
RF.1.3.b	Decode regularly spelled one-syllable words.
RF.1.3.c	Know final -e and common vowel team conventions for representing long vowel sounds.
RF.1.3.d	Use knowledge that every syllable must have a vowel sound to determine the number of syllables in a printed word.
RF.1.3.e	Decode two-syllable words following basic patterns by breaking the words into syllables.
RF.1.3.f	Read words with inflectional endings.
RF.1.3.g	Recognize and read grade-appropriate irregularly spelled words.
RF.1.4	Read with sufficient accuracy and fluency to support comprehension.
RF.1.4.a	Read grade-level text with purpose and understanding.
RF.1.4.b	Read grade-level text orally with accuracy, appropriate rate, and expression on successive readings.
RF.1.4.c	Use context to confirm or self-correct word recognition and understanding, rereading as necessary.

(continued)

KIT MATERIALS

- *Sentence Building Dominoes*: RF.1.1.a
- *Word Building Cubes*: RF.1.2.a, RF.1.2.b, RF.1.2.c, RF.1.2.d, RF.1.3.b, RF.1.3.c, RF.1.3.e
- *I Have...Who Has...? Interactive Game Cards*: RF.1.2.a
- *Big Box of Word Chunks*: RF.1.3.a, RF.1.3.b
- *SpinZone Magnetic Whiteboard Spinners*: RF.1.3.d, RF.1.3.g
- *Graphic Organizer Flip Chart*: RF.1.3.f, RF.1.4.a
- *Retell a Story Cubes*: RF.1.4.b
- *Parts of a Story Thumball*: RF.1.4.b
- *Write-on/Wipe-off Crayons*: RF.1.3.d, RF.1.3.g

CLASSROOM MATERIALS AND ACTIVITIES

- Classroom reading materials
- Magnetic letters
- Word walls

TIP FOR GENERALIZATION

Make phonics practice active! You can go outside and use sidewalk chalk to write several different letter blends on the concrete. Have students take turns tossing beanbags, then generating words that begin with that blend. For example, if the bean bag lands on "br-" the student can say "brown," "broom," etc. If you're unable to go outside, you can play the same game inside by using placing different papers with blends on them around the room. The activity can be modified to practice most of the target skills contained within this strand.

STUDENT: _____

RF.1.1* Actively engage in group reading activities with purpose and understanding.

*This standard is divided into one more specified standard: RF.1.1.a. Once this standard has been met, RF.1.1 is considered mastered.

RF.1.1.a Recognize the distinguishing features of a sentence (e.g., first word, capitalization, ending punctuation).

Materials: *Sentence Building Dominoes*

Teaching Procedure: Prior to the lesson, put dominoes into groups that can be used to create a sentence. For ease of organization, you may want to put them in cups or small resealable bags. Make sure that at least one domino starts with a capital letter and at least one domino shows punctuation. Challenge students to take their groups of dominoes and create a sentence. Depending on each student's current skill level, you may need to provide visual or verbal prompts to start each sentence with a capital letter, end with punctuation, etc. After each student has created a sentence, have them read the sentences aloud, then trade cups/bags of dominoes with one another.

"What's the rule for the first word of a sentence?" Point to a punctuation mark in text and ask, "What is this called?"

TARGET	INTRODUCED	MASTERED	GENERALIZATION PROBE	
Demonstrates knowledge that all sentences must start with a capital letter at least three times				
Demonstrates knowledge that all sentences must end with a punctuation mark at least three times				
When asked, points to a period				
When asked, points to a question mark				
When asked, points to an exclamation mark				
When provided with one example and one non-example of a sentence, correctly identifies the sentence and explains why the non-example is not a sentence				
Add additional targets				

 If your student has not met the prerequisite skills for this standard, drill down to RF.K.1 (RF.K.1.a–1.d).

 Procedure and Data Collection: Run 10–20 trials per session with a **Y** or **N** per trial. Graph the overall percentage of the number correct on the Per Opportunity Graph.

Mastery Criterion: 80% correct across three consecutive sessions with two different instructors.

STUDENT: _____

RF.1.2* Demonstrate understanding of spoken words, syllables, and sounds (phonemes).

*This standard is divided into four more specified standards: RF.1.2.a, RF.1.2.b, RF.1.2.c, and RF.1.2.d. Once these four standards have been met, RF.1.2 is considered mastered.

RF.1.2.a Distinguish long from short vowel sounds in spoken single-syllable words.

Materials: *I Have...Who Has...? Interactive Game Cards, Word Building Cubes,* Index cards (not included in kit)

Teaching Procedure: Mix up the blue and orange cards in the *I Have...Who Has...?* deck and then pass one to five cards out to each student. (Because cards correlate with one another, make sure that you have the correct cards in order to play the game. For example, one card says "I have the first card! Who has the word with the long 'a' sound for water falling from the sky?" You want to make sure a student or one of the teachers in the room has the card that says "rain.") Choose the number of cards students receive based on their ability to attend to multiple pieces of information simultaneously. After you have played through the cards you've given out, take all the cards back. Give each student one index card that says "LONG" and one index card that says "SHORT." Go back through the cards, reading the target word on each one aloud. After reading the target words, ask students to hold up the appropriate index card to describe if the vowel sound was long or short.

"Does ___ have a long 'a' or a short 'a' sound?" Name a single word and have students respond with "long" or "short."

TARGET	INTRODUCED	MASTERED	GENERALIZATION PROBE	
Consistently identifies the vowel in a written, single-syllable word for two or more vowels				
Consistently identifies the vowel in a written, single-syllable word for all five vowels				
Reads a written, single-syllable word aloud and identifies if the vowel sound is long or short for one or more vowels				
Reads a written, single-syllable word aloud and identifies if the vowel sound is long or short for three or more vowels				
Reads a written, single-syllable word aloud and identifies if the vowel sound is long or short for all five vowels				
Identifies if the vowel sound for a spoken word is long or short for one or more vowels				

(continued)

STUDENT: _____

(RF.1.2.a page 2)

Identifies if the vowel sound for a spoken word is long or short for three or more vowels				
Identifies if the vowel sound for a spoken word is long or short for all five vowels				
Add additional targets				

 If your student has not met the prerequisite skills for this standard, drill down to RF.K.2 (RF.K.2.a–2.e).

 Procedure and Data Collection: Run 10–20 trials per session with a **Y** or **N** per trial. Graph the overall percentage of the number correct on the Per Opportunity Graph.

Mastery Criterion: 80% correct across three consecutive sessions with two different instructors.

RF.1.2* Demonstrate understanding of spoken words, syllables, and sounds (phonemes).

**This standard is divided into four more specified standards: RF.1.2.a, RF.1.2.b, RF.1.2.c, and RF.1.2.d.
Once these four standards have been met, RF.1.2 is considered mastered.*

RF.1.2.b Orally produce single-syllable words by blending sounds (phonemes), including consonant blends.

Materials: *Word Building Cubes*

Teaching Procedure: Create words using the *Word Building Cubes*. Place a word on the table within view of the students and have them pronounce it. You can also allow students to create their own words and pronounce those.

"Can you say this word?" "How is this pronounced?" "What does this say?"

TARGET	INTRODUCED	MASTERED	GENERALIZATION PROBE	
After teacher sounds out each phoneme, blends sounds to pronounce word for at least 10 words				
After teacher sounds out each phoneme, blends sounds to pronounce word for at least 25 words				
After teacher sounds out each phoneme, blends sounds to pronounce word for at least 100 words				
Independently sounds out each phoneme, then blends sounds to pronounce word for at least 25 words				
Independently sounds out each phoneme, then blends sounds to pronounce word for at least 100 words				
Pronounces novel single-syllable words for at least 25 words				
Add additional targets				

If your student has not met the prerequisite skills for this standard, drill down to RF.K.2.b, RF.K.2.c.

Procedure and Data Collection: Run 10–20 trials per session with a **Y** or **N** per trial.
Graph the overall percentage of the number correct on the Per Opportunity Graph.

Mastery Criterion: 80% correct across three consecutive sessions with two different instructors.

STUDENT: _____

RF.1.2*

Demonstrate understanding of spoken words, syllables, and sounds (phonemes).

This standard is divided into four more specified standards: RF.1.2.a, RF.1.2.b, RF.1.2.c, and RF.1.2.d. Once these four standards have been met, RF.1.2 is considered mastered.

RF.1.2.c

Isolate and pronounce initial, medial vowel, and final sounds (phonemes) in spoken single-syllable words.

Materials: If your students initially require the use of visual prompts, you may consider using *Word Building Cubes*.

Teaching Procedure: If you are using the *Word Building Cubes*, have the necessary cubes prepared and easily accessible to you, but out of view of the students. Tell students what sound you are listening for. Say a word out loud, and then model how to isolate and pronounce the sound. For example, you may say, "What is the first sound in cat?" Then say, "cat," "c," "c," "cat." If you are using the *Word Building Cubes*, after you have modeled as described, place the word on the table and point to the "C" cube while saying "The sound in 'cat' is 'c.'" Remove the cubes, then introduce a new word and have students isolate and pronounce the sounds with you. After a couple rounds of guided practice, provide opportunities for individual students to isolate and pronounce the sounds independently.

"What is the first sound in the word ____?" "What vowel sound do you hear in the word ____?" "What are the sounds in the word ___?"

TARGET	INTRODUCED	MASTERED	GENERALIZATION PROBE	
Isolates and pronounces the first sound in a single-syllable word for five different words				
Isolates and pronounces the first sound in a single-syllable word for ten different words				
Isolates and pronounces the first sound in a single-syllable word for any novel word				
Isolates and pronounces the final sound in a single-syllable word for five different words				
Isolates and pronounces the final sound in a single-syllable word for ten different words				
Isolates and pronounces the final sound in a single-syllable word for any novel word				
Isolates and pronounces the vowel sound in a single-syllable word for five different words				
Isolates and pronounces the vowel sound in a single-syllable word for ten different words				
Isolates and pronounces the vowel sound in a single-syllable word for any novel word				

(continued)

Add additional targets				

⚠ **If your student has not met the prerequisite skills for this standard, drill down to RF.K.2.d.**

Procedure and Data Collection: Run 10–20 trials per session with a **Y** or **N** per trial. Graph the overall percentage of the number correct on the Per Opportunity Graph.

Mastery Criterion: 80% correct across three consecutive sessions with two different instructors.

STUDENT: _____

RF.1.2* Demonstrate understanding of spoken words, syllables, and sounds (phonemes).

**This standard is divided into four more specified standards: RF.1.2.a, RF.1.2.b, RF.1.2.c, and RF.1.2.d.
Once these four standards have been met, RF.1.2 is considered mastered.*

RF.1.2.d Segment spoken single-syllable words into their complete sequence of individual sounds (phonemes).

Materials: If your students initially require the use of visual prompts, you may consider using *Word Building Cubes.*

Teaching Procedure: If you are using the *Word Building Cubes*, have the necessary cubes prepared and easily accessible to you, but out of view of the students. Say a word the word out loud, then model how to isolate and pronounce the complete sequence of individual sounds. For example, say "cat," "/c/a/t/." If you are using the *Word Building Cubes*, after you have modeled as described, place the word on the table and point to the corresponding letter for each sound as you make it. Remove the cubes, and then introduce a new word and have students isolate and pronounce the sounds with you. After a couple rounds of guided practice, provide opportunities for individual students to isolate and pronounce the sounds independently.

"What are the sounds in the word ___?" "Tell me the phonemes that make the word ___?"

TARGET	INTRODUCED	MASTERED	GENERALIZATION PROBE	
Isolates and pronounces the complete sequence of individual sounds in a CVC word for five different CVC words				
Isolates and pronounces the complete sequence of individual sounds in a CVC word for 10 different CVC words				
Isolates and pronounces the complete sequence of individual sounds in a CVC word for any novel CVC word				
Isolates and pronounces the complete sequence of individual sounds in a single-syllable word for five different words that include blends and digraphs				
Isolates and pronounces the complete sequence of individual sounds in a single-syllable word for 10 different words that include blends and digraphs				
Isolates and pronounces the complete sequence of individual sounds in a single-syllable word for any novel word that include blends and digraphs				

(continued)

Add additional targets				

If your student has not met the prerequisite skills for this standard, drill down to RF.K.2.e.

Procedure and Data Collection: Run 10-20 trials per session with a **Y** or **N** per trial.
Graph the overall percentage of the number correct on the Per Opportunity Graph.

Mastery Criterion: 80% correct across three consecutive sessions with two different instructors.

STUDENT: _____

Reading/Foundational Skills
Phonics and Word Recognition
**RF.1.3: RF.1.3.a, RF.1.3.b, RF.1.3.c, RF.1.3.d,
RF.1.3.e, RF.1.3.f, RF.1.3.g**

RF.1.3*

Know and apply grade-level phonics and word analysis skills in decoding words.

This standard is divided into seven more specified standards: RF.1.3.a, RF.1.3.b, RF.1.3.c, RF.1.3.d, RF.1.3.e, RF.1.3.f, and RF.1.3.g. Once these seven standards have been met, RF.1.3 is considered mastered.

RF.1.3.a

Know the spelling-sound correspondences for common consonant digraphs.

Materials: *Big Box of Word Chunks*

Teaching Procedure: Place several puzzle pieces with consonant digraphs in view of the students. Pronounce a word, and then have the students find the correct consonant digraph. For example, you may put the puzzle pieces showing "sp," "str," and "tw" on the table. Say the word "street" and have the students identify "str" as the consonant digraph found in the word. You can then have students generate other words that begin with "str" before moving on to the next consonant digraph.

"What do you hear in the word ___?" "How do you spell the sound ___?"

TARGET	INTRODUCED	MASTERED	GENERALIZATION PROBE
Identifies the spelling-sound correspondence for five common consonant digraphs			
Identifies the spelling-sound correspondence for 10 common consonant digraphs			
Identifies the spelling-sound correspondence for 25 common consonant digraphs			
Add additional targets			

If your student has not met the prerequisite skills for this standard, drill down to RF.K.3.a.

Procedure and Data Collection: Run 10–20 trials per session with a **Y** or **N** per trial. Graph the overall percentage of the number correct on the Per Opportunity Graph.

Mastery Criterion: 80% correct across three consecutive sessions with two different instructors.

Reading/Foundational Skills
Phonics and Word Recognition
RF.1.3: RF.1.3.a, RF.1.3.b, RF.1.3.c, RF.1.3.d,
RF.1.3.e, RF.1.3.f, RF.1.3.g

STUDENT: _____

RF.1.3*

Know and apply grade-level phonics and word analysis skills in decoding words.

This standard is divided into seven more specified standards: RF.1.3.a, RF.1.3.b, RF.1.3.c, RF.1.3.d, RF.1.3.e, RF.1.3.f, and RF.1.3.g. Once these seven standards have been met, RF.1.3 is considered mastered.

RF.1.3.b

Decode regularly spelled one-syllable words.

Materials: *Word Building Cubes*, *Big Box of Word Chunks*

Teaching Procedure: Spell out a word using the *Word Building Cubes* for your students. Model how to decode the word. For example, say "cat," say "c/a/t/," then "cat." Introduce a new word to guide students through practice. Start with simple CVC words. Have them read the word, touching each letter cube as they make the sound, and then blending the sounds into one word. For students who are doing well with the skill, you can include the *Word Building Cubes* that show blends and digraphs.

"What does this word say?" "Can you decode this word?"

TARGET	INTRODUCED	MASTERED	GENERALIZATION PROBE	
Decodes at least 10 common CVC words				
Decodes at least 25 common CVC words				
Decodes at least 50 simple one-syllable words				
Decodes at least 10 one-syllable words that include blends and digraphs				
Decodes at least 25 one-syllable words that include blends and digraphs				
Decodes at least 50 one-syllable words that include blends and digraphs				
Decodes novel one-syllable words				
Add additional targets				

If your student has not met the prerequisite skills for this standard, drill down to RF.K.3 (RF.K.3.a–3.d).

Procedure and Data Collection: Run 10–20 trials per session with a **Y** or **N** per trial. Graph the overall percentage of the number correct on the Per Opportunity Graph.

Mastery Criterion: 80% correct across three consecutive sessions with two different instructors.

Reading/Foundational Skills
Phonics and Word Recognition
RF.1.3: RF.1.3.a, RF.1.3.b, RF.1.3.c, RF.1.3.d,
RF.1.3.e, RF.1.3.f, RF.1.3.g

STUDENT: _____

RF.1.3* Know and apply grade-level phonics and word analysis skills in decoding words.

This standard is divided into seven more specified standards: RF.1.3.a, RF.1.3.b, RF.1.3.c, RF.1.3.d, RF.1.3.e, RF.1.3.f, and RF.1.3.g. Once these seven standards have been met, RF.1.3 is considered mastered.

RF.1.3.c Know final -e and common vowel team conventions for representing long vowel sounds.

Materials: *Word Building Cubes*

Teaching Procedure: Introduce the "Magic e" Rule: when an "e" ends a word it is usually silent and makes the other vowel in the word say its own name (when there's no more than one letter between the other vowel and the "Magic e"). Use the *Word Building Cubes* to create a word within view of the students. Have students pronounce that word. Then, add an "e" to the end and have student pronounce the new word. For example, spell "cap" then add an "e" to spell "cape."

For vowel team conventions, introduce the rule "when two vowels go walking, the first one does the talking." You can use the vowel team cubes from the *Word Building Cubes* to practice vowel teams in isolation and then to practice them within words.

"What happens when I add an 'e' to the end of this word?" "How do you pronounce this word?"

TARGET	INTRODUCED	MASTERED	GENERALIZATION PROBE
Describes the "Magic e" rule when asked			
Adds an "e" to the end of a CVC word and correctly pronounces the new word for five words			
Adds an "e" to the end of a CVC word and correctly pronounces the new word for 10 words			
Adds an "e" to the end of a CVC word and correctly pronounces the new word for novel words			
Describes the vowel team rule when asked			
Correctly pronounces words for one vowel team (e.g., pronounces words containing "ai" with a long "a")			
Correctly pronounces words for three vowel teams			
Correctly pronounces words for all vowel teams that follow convention (i.e., ai, ea, ee, ei, ie, oa, oe, ue)			

(continued)

Reading/Foundational Skills
Phonics and Word Recognition
**RF.1.3: RF.1.3.a, RF.1.3.b, RF.1.3.c, RF.1.3.d,
RF.1.3.e, RF.1.3.f, RF.1.3.g**

STUDENT: _____

(RF.1.3.c page 2)

Add additional targets				

 If your student has not met the prerequisite skills for this standard, drill down to RF.K.3 (RF.K.3.a–3.d).

 Procedure and Data Collection: Run 10–20 trials per session with a **Y** or **N** per trial. Graph the overall percentage of the number correct on the Per Opportunity Graph.

Mastery Criterion: 80% correct across three consecutive sessions with two different instructors.

Reading/Foundational Skills
Phonics and Word Recognition
**RF.1.3: RF.1.3.a, RF.1.3.b, RF.1.3.c, RF.1.3.d,
RF.1.3.e, RF.1.3.f, RF.1.3.g**

STUDENT: _____

RF.1.3*

Know and apply grade-level phonics and word analysis skills in decoding words.

This standard is divided into seven more specified standards: RF.1.3.a, RF.1.3.b, RF.1.3.c, RF.1.3.d, RF.1.3.e, RF.1.3.f, and RF.1.3.g. Once these seven standards have been met, RF.1.3 is considered mastered.

RF.1.3.d

Use knowledge that every syllable must have a vowel sound to determine the number of syllables in a printed word.

Materials: *SpinZone Magnetic Whiteboard Spinners,* Write-on/Wipe-off Crayons

Teaching Procedure: Attach a spinner to the whiteboard. Draw a circle around it, then divide it into 8–12 parts for your lesson. In each part, write one word, making sure that the words vary in number of syllables. For example, you might divide the circle into 8 parts, then write one of the following words in each part: cat, zebra, elephant, dog, turtle, alligator, hamster, duck. Students take turns spinning the spinner and identifying the number of syllables in the word the spinner lands on. You can have students underline each vowel in the word to help determine the number of syllables. You can easily differentiate this activity by placing two or three spinners on the board and writing in words with varying levels of difficulty. For example, one spinner only contains one- and two-syllable words, while another spinner contains up to four-syllable words. Instruct students to spin a particular spinner based on their syllable ability. You can also include strategies such as clapping out syllables to support this skill.

"How many syllables does this word contain?" "Can you underline all the vowels in this word?"

TARGET	INTRODUCED	MASTERED	GENERALIZATION PROBE	
Underlines all the vowels in a printed word for one- to two-syllable words				
Divides a printed word into syllables, then checks that each syllable has a vowel for one- to two-syllable words				
Divides a printed word into syllables, then checks that each syllable has a vowel for three- or more syllable words				
Add additional targets				

If your student has not met the prerequisite skills for this standard, drill down to RF.K.3 (RF.K.3.a–3.d).

Procedure and Data Collection: Run 10–20 trials per session with a **Y** or **N** per trial. Graph the overall percentage of the number correct on the Per Opportunity Graph.

Mastery Criterion: 80% correct across three consecutive sessions with two different instructors.

Reading/Foundational Skills
Phonics and Word Recognition
**RF.1.3: RF.1.3.a, RF.1.3.b, RF.1.3.c, RF.1.3.d,
RF.1.3.e, RF.1.3.f, RF.1.3.g**

STUDENT: _____

RF.1.3* Know and apply grade-level phonics and word analysis skills in decoding words.

*This standard is divided into seven more specified standards: RF.1.3.a, RF.1.3.b, RF.1.3.c, RF.1.3.d, RF.1.3.e, RF.1.3.f, and RF.1.3.g. Once these seven standards have been met, RF.1.3 is considered mastered.

RF.1.3.e Decode two-syllable words following basic patterns by breaking the words into syllables.

Materials: *Word Building Cubes*

Teaching Procedure: Prior to the lesson, prepare a list of words or organize cubes for two-syllable words. Spell out a word using the *Word Building Cubes* for your students. Model how to decode the word. For example, spell "brother," say "br/o/th/e/r," then "brother." Introduce a new word to guide students through practice. Start with simple two-syllable words. Have them read the word, touching each letter cube as they make the sound, then blending the sounds into one word. For students who are doing well with the skill, you can include the *Word Building Cubes* that show blends and digraphs.

"What does this word say?" "Can you decode this word?"

TARGET	INTRODUCED	MASTERED	GENERALIZATION PROBE	
Decodes at least 10 common two-syllable words				
Decodes at least 25 common two-syllable words				
Decodes at least 50 simple two-syllable words				
Decodes at least 10 two-syllable words that include blends and digraphs				
Decodes at least 25 two-syllable words that include blends and digraphs				
Decodes at least 50 two-syllable words that include blends and digraphs				
Decodes novel two-syllable words				
Add additional targets				

If your student has not met the prerequisite skills for this standard, drill down to RF.K.3 (RF.K.3.a–3.d).

Procedure and Data Collection: Run 10–20 trials per session with a **Y** or **N** per trial. Graph the overall percentage of the number correct on the Per Opportunity Graph.

Mastery Criterion: 80% correct across three consecutive sessions with two different instructors.

Reading/Foundational Skills
Phonics and Word Recognition
**RF.1.3: RF.1.3.a, RF.1.3.b, RF.1.3.c, RF.1.3.d,
RF.1.3.e, RF.1.3.f, RF.1.3.g**

STUDENT: _____

RF.1.3* Know and apply grade-level phonics and word analysis skills in decoding words.

*This standard is divided into seven more specified standards: RF.1.3.a, RF.1.3.b, RF.1.3.c, RF.1.3.d, RF.1.3.e, RF.1.3.f, and RF.1.3.g. Once these seven standards have been met, RF.1.3 is considered mastered.

RF.1.3.f Read words with inflectional endings.

Materials: *Graphic Organizer Flip Chart*

Teaching Procedure: Use the "Four Column" page in the *Graphic Organizer Flip Chart Activity Book*, making sure you have a copy for each student. Label the first column "word," the second column "-s", the third column "-ed", and the fourth column "-ing." Provide an example of adding inflectional endings, such as filling in the chart with "cook," "cooks," "cooked," and "cooking" and providing a sample sentence for each word with the inflectional ending. Add another example and have students read each word in the chart. Have students generate their own words to complete their charts, then practice reading each set of words. You may want to focus on a small number of inflectional endings for one lesson, or devote one lesson to the inflectional endings "-s" and "-es."

"How do you pronounce this word?" "What does this say?" "Can you find the word that says ___?"

TARGET	INTRODUCED	MASTERED	GENERALIZATION PROBE
Reads words that contain the inflectional ending "-s" for at least 10 words			
Reads words that contain the inflectional ending "-s" for any novel words			
Reads words that contain the inflectional ending "-es" for at least 10 words			
Reads words that contain the inflectional ending "-es" for any novel words			
Reads words that contain the inflectional ending "-ed" for at least 10 words			
Reads words that contain the inflectional ending "-ed" for any novel words			
Reads words that contain the inflectional ending "-ing" for at least 10 words			
Reads words that contain the inflectional ending "-ing" for any novel words			

(continued)

Reading/Foundational Skills
Phonics and Word Recognition
**RF.1.3: RF.1.3.a, RF.1.3.b, RF.1.3.c, RF.1.3.d,
RF.1.3.e, RF.1.3.f, RF.1.3.g**

STUDENT: _____

(RF.1.3.f page 2)

Add additional targets				

 If your student has not met the prerequisite skills for this standard, drill down to RF.K.3 (RF.K.3.a–3.d).

 Procedure and Data Collection: Run 10–20 trials per session with a **Y** or **N** per trial. Graph the overall percentage of the number correct on the Per Opportunity Graph.

Mastery Criterion: 80% correct across three consecutive sessions with two different instructors.

Reading/Foundational Skills
Phonics and Word Recognition
**RF.1.3: RF.1.3.a, RF.1.3.b, RF.1.3.c, RF.1.3.d,
RF.1.3.e, RF.1.3.f, RF.1.3.g**

STUDENT: _____

RF.1.3* Know and apply grade-level phonics and word analysis skills in decoding words.

*This standard is divided into seven more specified standards: RF.1.3.a, RF.1.3.b, RF.1.3.c, RF.1.3.d, RF.1.3.e, RF.1.3.f, and RF.1.3.g. Once these seven standards have been met, RF.1.3 is considered mastered.

RF.1.3.g Recognize and read grade-appropriate irregularly spelled words.

Materials: : *SpinZone Magnetic Whiteboard Spinners, Write-on/Wipe-off Crayons*

Teaching Procedure: Attach a spinner to the whiteboard. Draw a circle around it, then divide it into the necessary number of parts for your lesson. The number of parts in the circle depends upon the number of irregularly spelled words you want to introduce to your students. First grade-appropriate irregularly spelled words include those such as again, said, friend, many, bear, water, and head. Students take turns spinning the spinner, then reading the word the spinner is pointing to. You can easily differentiate this activity by placing two or three spinners on the board and writing in varying numbers of words.

"What does this word say?" "Can you read this word?"

TARGET	INTRODUCED	MASTERED	GENERALIZATION PROBE	
Recognizes and reads at least five grade-appropriate irregularly spelled words				
Recognizes and reads at least 10 grade-appropriate irregularly spelled words				
Recognizes and reads at least 25 grade-appropriate irregularly spelled words				
Recognizes and reads all words on the First Grade Dolch Sight Words List				
Add additional targets				

  If your student has not met the prerequisite skills for this standard, drill down to RF.K.3 (RF.K.3.a – 3.d).

  Procedure and Data Collection: Run 10–20 trials per session with a **Y** or **N** per trial. Graph the overall percentage of the number correct on the Per Opportunity Graph.

Mastery Criterion: 80% correct across three consecutive sessions with two different instructors.

STUDENT: _____

RF.1.4*

Read with sufficient accuracy and fluency to support comprehension.

*This standard is divided into three more specified standards: R.F.1.4.a, R.F.1.4.b, and R.F.1.4.c. Once these three standards have been met, RF.1.4 is considered mastered.

RF.1.4.a

Read grade-level text with purpose and understanding.

Materials: *Graphic Organizer Flip Chart,* Classroom reading materials

Teaching Procedure: Use the "Story Map" or the "5 W's" graphics from the *Graphic Organizer Flip Chart.* During and/or after a reading activity, ask questions to check for understanding and put responses in the appropriate spaces on the graphic organizer.

"Time to read." "Who is the main character?" "How was the problem solved?" "When did the main character ___?"

TARGET	INTRODUCED	MASTERED	GENERALIZATION PROBE	
Responds correctly to questions checking for understanding about three different grade-level texts in 80% of opportunities				
Responds correctly to questions checking for understanding about a novel text in 80% of opportunities				
With prompting and support, chooses a variety of appropriate-level texts to read during independent reading or breaks				
Independently chooses a variety of appropriate-level texts to read during independent reading or breaks				
Responds correctly to questions checking for understanding after reading independently in 80% of opportunities				
Add additional targets				

 If your student has not met the prerequisite skills for this standard, drill down to RF.K.4.

 Procedure and Data Collection: Run 10–20 trials per session with a **Y** or **N** per trial. Graph the overall percentage of the number correct on the Per Opportunity Graph.

Mastery Criterion: 80% correct across three consecutive sessions with two different instructors.

STUDENT: _____

RF.1.4*

Read with sufficient accuracy and fluency to support comprehension.

*This standard is divided into three more specified standards: R.F.1.4.a, R.F.1.4.b, and R.F.1.4.c.
Once these three standards have been met, RF.1.4 is considered mastered.*

RF.1.4.b

Read grade-level text orally with accuracy, appropriate rate, and expression on successive readings.

Materials: *Retell a Story Cubes, Parts of a Story Thumball,* Storybooks or other classroom reading materials

Teaching Procedure: Create a clear routine for starting independent reading activities. This can include audio or visual cues that a transition is about to take place. Make sure that your students understand how to choose appropriately leveled books. After each student is done reading, let students take turns throwing the *Parts of a Story Thumball* or rolling the *Retell a Story Cubes* and responding to additional questions to check for understanding.

"Read with expression." "Can you read faster?" "Read it again." "Let's pronounce that word one more time."

TARGET	INTRODUCED	MASTERED	GENERALIZATION PROBE	
Reads appropriate-level text aloud to teacher for three different texts, accurately pronouncing at least 90% of the words				
Reads appropriate-level text aloud when presented with a novel text, accurately pronouncing at least 90% of the words				
Increases percentage of accurately pronounced words with successive readings of the same text				
Reads appropriate-level text aloud to teacher for three different texts, reading at an appropriate rate (60-80 words per minute)				
Reads appropriate-level text aloud to teacher for a novel text, reading at an appropriate rate (60-80 words per minute)				
Increases rate with successive readings of the same text				
Reads aloud with expression for an appropriate-level text for three different texts				
Reads aloud with expression for an appropriate-level text when presented with a novel text				
Increases accuracy, rate of reading, and expression on successive readings of the same text				

(continued)

STUDENT: _____

(RF.1.4.b page 2)

Add additional targets				

 If your student has not met the prerequisite skills for this standard, drill down to RF.K.4.

 Procedure and Data Collection: Run 10–20 trials per session with a **Y** or **N** per trial.
Graph the overall percentage of the number correct on the Per Opportunity Graph.

Mastery Criterion: 80% correct across three consecutive sessions with two different instructors.

STUDENT: _____

RF.1.4* Read with sufficient accuracy and fluency to support comprehension.

*This standard is divided into three more specified standards: R.F.1.4.a, R.F.1.4.b, and R.F.1.4.c.
Once these three standards have been met, RF.1.4 is considered mastered.

RF.1.4.c Use context to confirm or self-correct word recognition and understanding, rereading as necessary.

Materials: Storybooks or other classroom reading materials

Teaching Procedure: Based on student performance on other foundational skills such as decoding, choose reading materials that address deficits. For example, if you see that your student is struggling with correctly decoding CVC-e words, choose reading materials to practice that skill. Sit with the student as he/she reads a sentence aloud, then provide prompts as needed to help the student self-correct.

"Is that how you say that word?" "Does the sentence make sense the way you read it?" "Try again."

TARGET	INTRODUCED	MASTERED	GENERALIZATION PROBE	
Upon making an error, self-corrects word recognition for familiar words based on context when reading a single sentence for at least 80% of opportunities				
Upon making an error, self-corrects word recognition for familiar words based on context when reading a three to five sentence paragraph for at least 80% of opportunities				
Upon making an error, self-corrects word recognition for novel words based on context when reading a single sentence paragraph for at least 80% of opportunities				
Upon making an error, self-corrects word recognition for novel words based on context when reading a three to five sentence paragraph for at least 80% of opportunities				
Add additional targets				

If your student has not met the prerequisite skills for this standard, drill down to RF.K.4.

Procedure and Data Collection: Run 10–20 trials per session with a **Y** or **N** per trial. Graph the overall percentage of the number correct on the Per Opportunity Graph.

Mastery Criterion: 80% correct across three consecutive sessions with two different instructors.

STRAND
Writing

WRITING OVERVIEW

• Share opinions, information, and narrative through writing
• Utilize digital tools to organize and share information
• Participate in conversations with both peers and adults to share and improve writing

CCSS CODE	STANDARD
W.1.1	Write opinion pieces in which they introduce the topic or name the book they are writing about, state an opinion, supply a reason for the opinion, and provide some sense of closure.
W.1.2	Write informative/explanatory texts in which they name a topic, supply some facts about the topic, and provide some sense of closure.
W.1.3	Write narratives in which they recount two or more appropriately sequenced events, include some details regarding what happened, use temporal words to signal event order, and provide some sense of closure.
W.1.5	With guidance and support from adults, focus on a topic, respond to questions and suggestions from peers, and add details to strengthen writing as needed.
W.1.6	With guidance and support from adults, use a variety of digital tools to produce and publish writing, including in collaboration with peers.
W.1.7	Participate in shared research and writing projects (e.g., explore a number of "how-to" books on a given topic and use them to write a sequence of instructions).
W.1.8	With guidance and support from adults, recall information from experiences or gather information from provided sources to answer a question.

Note: W.1.4 begins in grade 3, W.1.9 begins in grade 4, W.1.10 begins in grade 3.

KIT MATERIALS

• *Graphic Organizer Flip Chart*: W.1.1, W.1.2, W.1.5, W.1.7, W.1.8
• *Writing Prompts Cards*: W.1.2, W.1.5, W.1.7, W.1.8
• *Speaker's Box*: W.1.3

CLASSROOM MATERIALS AND ACTIVITIES

• Handwriting paper
• Classroom art supplies
• Tablet apps such as Snapguide, Flowboard, or SketchNotes can be used as digital tools for producing and publishing writing

TIP FOR GENERALIZATION

During a field trip or community walk, have students take pictures using smartphones, tablets, or cameras. After returning to the classroom, students can write about the trip using their pictures as a guide.

W.1.1 Write opinion pieces in which they introduce the topic or name the book they are writing about, state an opinion, supply a reason for the opinion, and provide some sense of closure.

Materials: *Graphic Organizer Flip Chart,* Handwriting paper/student notebooks, Classroom reading materials

Teaching Procedure: Provide students with paper and access to the book or reading materials they will be writing about. Based on the student's individual skill level, provide a specific question that he/she should be addressing. You may want to provide a choice of questions they can respond to. Utilize the "Hamburger" page in the *Graphic Organizer Flip Chart Activity Book* (make sure each student has a copy) to help students organize their thoughts before writing the opinion piece. Each piece of the hamburger should be clearly labeled to help students identify what information belongs there, such as labeling the top bun "Introduce topic," the tomato as "State your opinion," and so on.

"Tell me what you thought about this book." "Would you recommend this book to another person?" "Do you think the character made the right choice?"

TARGET	INTRODUCED	MASTERED	GENERALIZATION PROBE
With prompting and support, writes a sentence introducing the topic or book being discussed			
Independently writes a sentence introducing the topic or book being discussed			
With prompting and support, states an opinion in response to a direct question for three different topics or books			
Independently states an opinion in response to a direct question for three different topics or books			
Independently states an opinion in response to a direct question for three to five novel topics or books			
Independently writes an opinion in response to a written or oral direct question			
With prompting and support, supplies a reason for an opinion for three different topics or books			
Independently supplies a reason for an opinion for three different topics or books			
Independently supplies a reason for an opinion for three to five novel topics or books			
Independently writes a reason for an opinion			

(continued)

STUDENT: _____

(W.1.1 page 2)

With prompting and support, writes a closing sentence for an opinion piece				
Independently writes a closing sentence for an opinion piece				
With prompting and support, completes all parts of an opinion piece for one topic or book				
Independently completes all parts of an opinion piece for any topic or book				
Add additional targets				

 If your student has not met the prerequisite skills for this standard, drill down to W.K.1.

 Procedure and Data Collection: Run 10–20 trials per session with a **Y** or **N** per trial. Graph the overall percentage of the number correct on the Per Opportunity Graph.

Mastery Criterion: 80% correct across three consecutive sessions with two different instructors.

W.1.2

Write informative/explanatory texts in which they name a topic, supply some facts about the topic, and provide some sense of closure.

Materials: *Writing Prompts Cards, Graphic Organizer Flip Chart,* Handwriting paper/student notebooks

Teaching Procedure: Select topics from the Expository category in the *Writing Prompts Cards.* You can select one topic for all students, or provide two to three choices for each student. Each card provides several questions and suggestions for writing about the topic. You may want to utilize a graphic from the *Graphic Organizer Flip Chart* to help students organize their thoughts before writing.

"Tell me something else about ___." "Can you write a topic sentence?"

TARGET	INTRODUCED	MASTERED	GENERALIZATION PROBE	
With prompting and support, writes a sentence introducing the topic being discussed				
Independently writes a sentence introducing the topic being discussed				
With prompting and support, supplies one fact about the topic				
Independently supplies one fact about the topic				
With prompting and support, supplies at least three facts about the topic				
Independently supplies at least three facts about the topic				
With prompting and support, writes a closing sentence for an informative/explanatory piece				
Independently writes a closing sentence for an informative/explanatory piece				
With prompting and support, completes all parts of an informative/explanatory piece for one topic				
Independently completes all parts of an informative/ explanatory piece for any topic				
Add additional target				

⚠ **If your student has not met the prerequisite skills for this standard, drill down to W.K.2.**

Procedure and Data Collection: Run 10–20 trials per session with a **Y** or **N** per trial. Graph the overall percentage of the number correct on the Per Opportunity Graph.

Mastery Criterion: 80% correct across three consecutive sessions with two different instructors.

STUDENT: _____

W.1.3

Write narratives in which they recount two or more appropriately sequenced events, include some details regarding what happened, use temporal words to signal event order, and provide some sense of closure.

Materials: *Speaker's Box,* Handwriting paper/student notebooks

Teaching Procedure: Use the black "What's Happening Here?/What Comes Next?" cards from the *Speaker's Box.* Have students look at the pictures and choose their own card or have them randomly select a card from the box. Provide prompts as necessary to help students write a short narrative about the picture. Ask them to describe what is happening in the picture, what might happen next, and what might have happened before.

"Can you write about what's happening/happened?" "What kind of word will you use to tell me it happened yesterday?" "What's a good way to end your story?"

TARGET	INTRODUCED	MASTERED	GENERALIZATION PROBE	
Writes two sentences in appropriate sequence for three different narratives				
Writes two sentences in appropriate sequence for five different narratives				
Writes two sentences in appropriate sequence for a novel narrative				
Writes four to five sentences in appropriate sequence for three different narratives				
Writes four to five sentences in appropriate sequence for five different narratives				
Writes four to five sentences in appropriate sequence for a novel narrative				
Uses at least one temporal word/phrase (such as "next," "at first," etc.) in each narrative				
Uses two to three temporal words/phrases in each narrative				
With prompting and support, writes a final sentence that provides a sense of closure				
Independently writes a final sentence that provides a sense of closure				

(continued)

Add additional targets				

 If your student has not met the prerequisite skills for this standard, drill down to W.K.3.

 Procedure and Data Collection: Run 10–20 trials per session with a **Y** or **N** per trial. Graph the overall percentage of the number correct on the Per Opportunity Graph.

Mastery Criterion: 80% correct across three consecutive sessions with two different instructors.

STUDENT: _____

W.1.5   With guidance and support from adults, focus on a topic, respond to questions and suggestions from peers, and add details to strengthen writing as needed.

Materials: *Writing Prompts Cards,* *Graphic Organizer Flip Chart,* Handwriting paper/student notebooks

Teaching Procedure: Select topics from the Journal, Descriptive, or Narrative categories in the *Writing Prompts Cards.* You can select one topic for all students, or provide two to three choices for each student. Each topic card provides several questions and suggestions for writing about the topic. You may want to utilize a graphic from the *Graphic Organizer Flip Chart* to help students organize their thoughts before writing.

"Can you add a sentence about ___?" "Listen to the question." "Can you ask a peer for feedback?"

TARGET	INTRODUCED	MASTERED	GENERALIZATION PROBE	
Responds to questions about a written piece from the teacher				
Responds to one question about a written piece from one peer				
Responds to three questions about a written piece from one peer				
Responds to three questions about a written piece from two or more peers				
Listens to a suggestion for a written piece from the teacher and makes one change/addition to strengthen the piece				
Listens to a suggestion for a written piece from one peer and makes one change/addition to strengthen the piece				
Listens to a suggestion for a written piece from two or more peers and makes one change/addition to strengthen the piece				
Add additional targets				

   If your student has not met the prerequisite skills for this standard, drill down to W.K.5.

   Procedure and Data Collection: Run 10–20 trials per session with a **Y** or **N** per trial. Graph the overall percentage of the number correct on the Per Opportunity Graph.

Mastery Criterion: 80% correct across three consecutive sessions with two different instructors.

STUDENT: _____

W.1.6 With guidance and support from adults, use a variety of digital tools to produce and publish writing, including in collaboration with peers.

Materials: Computers, tablets, cameras (not included in kit)

Teaching Procedure: Introduce the computer program or tablet app that students will utilize to produce and publish writing. Include step-by-step instructions for using the program or app appropriately to complete the assigned task.

"Use ___ (program or app) to write your piece." "Work together to add a caption to the picture."

TARGET	INTRODUCED	MASTERED	GENERALIZATION PROBE
Uses computer or tablet program appropriately to complete a writing activity with 1:1 instruction from a teacher			
Uses computer or tablet program appropriately to complete a writing activity in group instruction			
Uses computer or tablet program appropriately and independently to complete a writing activity			
Shares computer or tablet program appropriately with one peer to collaborate on a writing activity for at least one activity			
Shares computer or tablet program appropriately with one peer to collaborate on a writing activity for at least three different activities			
Shares computer or tablet program appropriately with at least three peers to collaborate on a writing activity for at least three different activities			
Add additional targets			

If your student has not met the prerequisite skills for this standard, drill down to W.K.6.

Procedure and Data Collection: Run 10–20 trials per session with a **Y** or **N** per trial. Graph the overall percentage of the number correct on the Per Opportunity Graph.

Mastery Criterion: 80% correct across three consecutive sessions with two different instructors.

STUDENT: _____

W.1.7 Participate in shared research and writing projects (e.g., explore a number of "how-to" books on a given topic and use them to write a sequence of instructions).

Materials: *Writing Prompts Cards, Graphic Organizer Flip Chart,* Handwriting paper/student notebooks

Teaching Procedure: Select topics from the Expository category in the *Writing Prompts Cards.* You can select one topic for all students, or provide two to three choices for each student. Each card provides several questions and suggestions for writing about the topic. You may want to utilize a graphic from the *Graphic Organizer Flip Chart* to help students organize their thoughts before writing.

S^D "What did you learn from your research?" "Can you share one interesting fact?" "Describe how you make a ___."

TARGET	INTRODUCED	MASTERED	GENERALIZATION PROBE	
Reads at least two resources as research on an assigned topic				
Reads three or more resources as research on an assigned topic				
With prompting and support, shares one detail about research				
With prompting and support, shares three details about research				
Independently shares one detail about research				
Independently writes one detail about research				
Independently writes three details about research				
With prompting and support, writes information in the appropriate sequence				
Independently writes information in the appropriate sequence				
Add additional targets				

 If your student has not met the prerequisite skills for this standard, drill down to W.K.7.

 Procedure and Data Collection: Run 10-20 trials per session with a **Y** or **N** per trial. Graph the overall percentage of the number correct on the Per Opportunity Graph.

Mastery Criterion: 80% correct across three consecutive sessions with two different instructors.

STUDENT: _____

 W.1.8 With guidance and support from adults, recall information from experiences or gather information from provided sources to answer a question.

 Materials: *Writing Prompts Cards, Graphic Organizer Flip Chart,* Handwriting paper/student notebooks

 Teaching Procedure: Select topics from the Narrative category in the *Writing Prompts Cards.* You can select one topic for all students, or provide two to three choices for each student. Each card provides several questions and suggestions for writing about the topic. You may want to utilize a graphic from the *Graphic Organizer Flip Chart* to help students organize their thoughts before writing.

S^D "Tell me about what happened." "Can you write your story?" "Write a story about our field trip."

TARGET	INTRODUCED	MASTERED	GENERALIZATION PROBE	
Recalls experience from within the last 2 hours to respond to a novel question and write a response				
Recalls experience from within the last day to respond to a novel question and write a response				
Recalls experience from within the last week to respond to a novel question and write a response				
Recalls experience and writes at least three sentences about it				
With prompting and support, refers to another resource to gather more information to answer a question				
Add additional targets				

 If your student has not met the prerequisite skills for this standard, drill down to W.K.8.

 Procedure and Data Collection: Run 10–20 trials per session with a **Y** or **N** per trial. Graph the overall percentage of the number correct on the Per Opportunity Graph.

Mastery Criterion: 80% correct across three consecutive sessions with two different instructors.

SPEAKING AND LISTENING OVERVIEW

- Participate in collaborative conversation with a variety of partners about a variety of subjects
- Ask and answer questions to gain information, clear up confusion, and retell stories and events
- Use language to provide details and express ideas clearly

CCSS CODE	STANDARD
SL.1.1	Participate in collaborative conversations with diverse partners about grade 1 topics and texts with peers and adults in small and larger groups.
SL.1.1.a	Follow agreed-upon rules for discussions (e.g., listening to others with care, speaking one at a time about the topics and texts under discussion).
SL.1.1.b	Build on others' talk in conversations by responding to the comments of others through multiple exchanges.
SL.1.1.c	Ask questions to clear up any confusion about the topics and texts under discussion.
SL.1.2	Ask and answer questions about key details in a text read aloud or information presented orally or through other media.
SL.1.3	Ask and answer questions about what a speaker says in order to gather additional information or clarify something that is not understood.
SL.1.4	Describe people, places, things, and events with relevant details, expressing ideas and feelings clearly.
SL.1.5	Add drawings or other visual displays to descriptions when appropriate to clarify ideas, thoughts, and feelings.
SL.1.6	Produce complete sentences when appropriate to task and situation.

KIT MATERIALS

- *Speaker's Box*: SL.1.1.b, SL.1.1.c, SL.1.3, SL.1.4
- *SpinZone Magnetic Whiteboard Spinners*: SL.1.2
- *Talking in Sentences*: SL.1.2, SL.1.4, SL.1.6

CLASSROOM MATERIALS AND ACTIVITIES

- Classroom writing materials (paper, pencils, markers)
- Visual cue for conversation, such as a "talking stick"
- Photos from newspapers or other publications
- Photos from field trips or other activities the class has engaged in

(continued)

TIP FOR GENERALIZATION

A quick and simple game you can play to practice basic conversation skills is the "I'm thinking of..." game. Tell your students that you are thinking of something, and have them ask questions to try to figure out what it is. You can utilize paraprofessionals or assistant teachers to prompt appropriate questions if necessary. Once your students have mastered guessing, you can allow students to be the "thinker."

SL.1.1* Participate in collaborative conversations with diverse partners about grade 1 topics and texts with peers and adults in small and larger groups.

This standard is divided into three more specified standards: SL.1.1.a, SL.1.1.b, and SL.1.1.c. Once these three standards have been met, SL.1.1 is considered mastered.

SL.1.1.a Follow agreed-upon rules for discussions (e.g., listening to others with care, speaking one at a time about the topics and texts under discussion).

Materials: Pictures from the newspaper, magazines, or classroom activities

Teaching Procedure: Introduce a picture, then pose a question or topic to start the conversation. You may want to include a visual cue of some sort, such as a talking stick, to help students take turns appropriately. After conversation is complete, you can select a new topic to continue the activity or encourage students to transition the conversation to a similar topic. For example, if the conversation is about a field trip the class took, you can transition to a conversation about ideas for future field trips.

"Can you remind me about the rules before we start?" A gesture such as placing your fingers to your lips or holding out a palm to indicate to wait before speaking. Receiving a "talking stick" or other visual prompt that indicates it's the student's turn to speak.

TARGET	INTRODUCED	MASTERED	GENERALIZATION PROBE	
Takes turns during conversation				
Attends to speaker for 80% of the time during a conversation				
Does not interrupt a speaker in eight out of 10 trials				
Adds at least one on-topic comment to the conversation				
Add additional targets				

If your student has not met the prerequisite skills for this standard, drill down to SL.K.1.a.

Procedure and Data Collection: Run 10-20 trials per session with a **Y** or **N** per trial. Graph the overall percentage of the number correct on the Per Opportunity Graph.

Mastery Criterion: 80% correct across three consecutive sessions with two different instructors.

SL.1.1* Participate in collaborative conversations with diverse partners about grade 1 topics and texts with peers and adults in small and larger groups.

*This standard is divided into three more specified standards: SL.1.1.a, SL.1.1.b, and SL.1.1.c.
Once these three standards have been met, SL.1.1 is considered mastered.

SL.1.1.b Build on others' talk in conversations by responding to the comments of others through multiple exchanges.

Materials: *Speaker's Box*

Teaching Procedure: Use the blue "Things You Like Best" cards from the *Speaker's Box.* Allow students to choose one card they want to discuss. The student should read the card aloud, and then respond. Prompt other students as necessary to continue in the conversation.

"What do you think?" "Does anyone have any questions?"

TARGET	INTRODUCED	MASTERED	GENERALIZATION PROBE	
Responds to at least one question from a teacher to build on conversation				
Responds to at least one question from a peer to build on conversation				
Provides an on-topic response to at least one comment from a teacher to build on conversation				
Provides an on-topic response to at least one comment from a peer to build on conversation				
Asks at least one on-topic question to build on conversation with a teacher				
Asks at least one on-topic question to build on conversation with a peer				
Asks at least one on-topic question to build on conversation with a small group				
Asks two to three on-topic questions to build on conversation with a teacher				
Asks two to three on-topic questions to build on conversation with a peer				
Asks two to three on-topic questions to build on conversation with a small group				
Asks on-topic questions to build on conversation with a variety of conversation partners				

(continued)

STUDENT: _____

(SL.1.1.b page 2)

Add additional targets				

⚠ **If your student has not met the prerequisite skills for this standard, drill down to SL.K.1.b.**

Procedure and Data Collection: Run 10–20 trials per session with a **Y** or **N** per trial.
Graph the overall percentage of the number correct on the Per Opportunity Graph.

Mastery Criterion: 80% correct across three consecutive sessions with two different instructors.

STUDENT: _____

SL.1.1* Participate in collaborative conversations with diverse partners about grade 1 topics and texts with peers and adults in small and larger groups.

*This standard is divided into three more specified standards: SL.1.1.a, SL.1.1.b, and SL.1.1.c. Once these three standards have been met, SL.1.1 is considered mastered.

SL.1.1.c Ask questions to clear up any confusion about the topics and texts under discussion.

 Materials: *Speaker's Box,* Classroom reading materials, Pictures from newspapers or other sources

 Teaching Procedure: Introduce a topic by using a card from the *Speaker's Box*, a picture from another source, or a classroom text. Provide students with textual prompts if necessary (e.g., an index card that says "What...." as a prompt to ask a question beginning with "What").

 "Does anyone have any questions?" Presentation of unknown item or image.

TARGET	INTRODUCED	MASTERED	GENERALIZATION PROBE	
Indicates verbally that clarification is needed (i.e., "I don't understand.")				
Consistently asks "what" questions to obtain more information from an adult during classroom reading and discussion activities				
Asks "what" questions to obtain more information from a peer during classroom reading and discussion activities				
Consistently asks "who" and "where" questions to obtain more information from an adult during classroom reading and discussion activities				
Asks "who" and "where" questions to obtain more information from a peer during classroom reading and discussion activities				
Consistently asks all wh- and "how" questions to obtain more information from an adult during classroom reading and discussion activities				
Asks all wh- and "how" questions to obtain more information from a peer during classroom reading and discussion activities				

(continued)

STUDENT: _____

(SL.1.1.c page 2)

Add additional targets				

 If your student has not met the prerequisite skills for this standard, drill down to SL.K.1.b, SL.K.2, SL.K.3.

 Procedure and Data Collection: Run 10–20 trials per session with a **Y** or **N** per trial.
Graph the overall percentage of the number correct on the Per Opportunity Graph.

Mastery Criterion: 80% correct across three consecutive sessions with two different instructors.

STUDENT: _____

SL.1.2   Ask and answer questions about key details in a text read aloud or information presented orally or through other media.

Materials: *Talking in Sentences, SpinZone Magnetic Whiteboard Spinners,* Classroom reading materials

Teaching Procedure: Select that day's lesson in *Talking in Sentences* and be sure to read through prior to teaching. Place the book flat on the table or make photocopies so that you can easily read the text while the picture is in full view of your students. Read the introduction, then take your students through the Listen and Respond, Talk About, and Let's Talk sections of the book.

"What is her name?" "What did ___ do when that happened?"

TARGET	INTRODUCED	MASTERED	GENERALIZATION PROBE	
Consistently responds to "who," "what," and "where" questions about a text read aloud or information presented orally				
Consistently responds to a random rotation of all five wh- questions about a text read aloud or information presented orally				
Responds with one fact to "What did you learn from the text?" after a text is read aloud or information is presented orally				
Responds with two to three facts to "What did you learn from the text?" after a text is read aloud or information is presented orally				
With prompting and support, generates one question about a text read aloud or information presented orally for three or more opportunities				
Independently generates one question about a text read aloud or information presented orally for three or more opportunities				
With prompting and support, generates two to three questions about a text read aloud or information presented orally for three or more opportunities				
Independently generates two to three questions about a text read aloud or information presented orally for three or more opportunities				

(continued)

STUDENT: _____

(SL.1.2 page 2)

Add additional targets				

If your student has not met the prerequisite skills for this standard, drill down to SL.K.2.

Procedure and Data Collection: Run 10–20 trials per session with a **Y** or **N** per trial.
Graph the overall percentage of the number correct on the Per Opportunity Graph.

Mastery Criterion: 80% correct across three consecutive sessions with two different instructors.

STUDENT: _____

SL.1.3   Ask and answer questions about what a speaker says in order to gather additional information or clarify something that is not understood.

Materials: *Appendix B: Encouraging Social Interactions and Conversations, Speaker's Box*

Teaching Procedure: During the course of the day, contrive opportunities for brief conversations with students to measure their progress in asking and answering questions about what a speaker says. Utilize the lists in Appendix B to prepare leading statements to teach students how to ask questions.

Note: If your student is not able to meet any of the prerequisite skills for this standard, you should assess using the VB-MAPP and start with developmentally appropriate goals.

Providing a leading statement such as "I did something really fun yesterday!"

TARGET	INTRODUCED	MASTERED	GENERALIZATION PROBE	
Indicates verbally that clarification is needed (i.e., "I don't understand.")				
Asks "what" questions to obtain more information when provided with a leading statement from an adult speaker				
Asks "who" and "where" questions to obtain more information when provided with a leading statement from an adult speaker				
Asks wh- questions appropriately from both peer and adult speakers to seek help, obtain information, or clarify				
Accurately responds when a teacher checks for understanding about a single-step direction (e.g., "What are we doing next?")				
Accurately responds when a teacher checks for understanding about a multiple-step direction				
Accurately responds when a teacher checks for understanding about a text read aloud or information presented orally				
Add additional target				

If your student has not met the prerequisite skills for this standard, drill down to SL.K.3.

Procedure and Data Collection: Run 10–20 trials per session with a **Y** or **N** per trial. Graph the overall percentage of the number correct on the Per Opportunity Graph.

Mastery Criterion: 80% correct across three consecutive sessions with two different instructors.

STUDENT: _____

SL.1.4   Describe people, places, things, and events with relevant details, expressing ideas and feelings clearly.

Materials: *Talking in Sentences, Speaker's Box,* Classroom reading materials, Pictures of familiar people, places, things, or events from the student's life

Teaching Procedure: Select that day's lesson in *Talking in Sentences* and be sure to read through prior to teaching. Place the book flat on the table or make photocopies so that you can easily read the text while the picture is in full view of your students. Read the introduction, then take your students through the Listen and Respond, Talk About, and Let's Talk sections of the book. You can also create specific questions in advance to use with pictures of your student's favorite people, places and things if your student struggles with this skill.

"Tell me about ___." "What happened after ___?" "Can you tell me more about that?"

TARGET	INTRODUCED	MASTERED	GENERALIZATION PROBE	
Provides one characteristic when describing a person				
Provides two characteristics when describing a person				
Provides three or more characteristics when describing a person, including how the person feels				
Uses a variety of descriptors when describing people (e.g., describes hair color for one person, height for another, the color of a shirt for a third)				
Provides one characteristic when describing a place or thing				
Provides two characteristics when describing a place or thing				
Provides three or more characteristics when describing a place or thing				
Uses a variety of descriptors when describing places and things				
Provides one characteristic when describing an event				
Provides two characteristics when describing an event				
Provides three or more characteristics when describing an event, including feelings and ideas related to the event				
Uses a variety of descriptors when describing events				

(continued)

Add additional targets				
			.	

If your student has not met the prerequisite skills for this standard, drill down to SL.K.4.

Procedure and Data Collection: Run 10–20 trials per session with a **Y** or **N** per trial.
Graph the overall percentage of the number correct on the Per Opportunity Graph.

Mastery Criterion: 80% correct across three consecutive sessions with two different instructors.

STUDENT: _____

SL.1.5

Add drawings or other visual displays to descriptions when appropriate to clarify ideas, thoughts, and feelings.

Materials: Classroom art supplies such as paper, pencils, and crayons (not included in kit)

Teaching Procedure: After the student has provided a verbal description of an item, person, or activity, ask them to show you what it looks like or to draw a particular detail about their description. For many learners with developmental disabilities, it may be difficult to connect a drawing to a conversation, so prompts and redirection may be necessary.

"Can you show me what it looks like?" "Draw it."

TARGET	INTRODUCED	MASTERED	GENERALIZATION PROBE	
Draws picture of a person, place, thing, or event that includes descriptors shared verbally (e.g., the student describes a boy holding a ball, then draws a picture that includes the boy holding the ball)				
Responds to questions from adults to provide further detail about a drawing				
Responds to questions from peers to provide further detail about a drawing				
Selects a variety of visual displays for conveying ideas, thoughts, and feelings (e.g., adds a drawing when appropriate to one description, adds a model made from clay for another description)				
Add additional targets				

If your student has not met the prerequisite skills for this standard, drill down to SL.K.5.

Procedure and Data Collection: Run 10–20 trials per session with a **Y** or **N** per trial. Graph the overall percentage of the number correct on the Per Opportunity Graph.

Mastery Criterion: 80% correct across three consecutive sessions with two different instructors.

STUDENT: _____

SL.1.6 Produce complete sentences when appropriate to task and situation.

Materials: *Talking in Sentences*

Teaching Procedure: Select that day's lesson in *Talking in Sentences* and be sure to read through prior to teaching. Place the book flat on the table or make photocopies so that you can easily read the text while the picture is in full view of your students. Read the introduction, then take your students through the Listen and Respond, Talk About, and Let's Talk sections of the book.

Note: If your student is not able to meet any of the prerequisite skills for this standard, you should assess using the VB-MAPP and start with developmentally appropriate goals.

"Say the whole thing." "Tell me in a complete sentence that starts with the words 'The girl.'" "What happened in the story?"

TARGET	INTRODUCED	MASTERED	GENERALIZATION PROBE	
With prompting and support, responds to a question with a simple noun-verb sentence (e.g., "The girl jumped.")				
Independently responds to questions with a simple noun-verb sentence				
With prompting and support, responds to a question with a sentence including appropriate use of linking verbs (e.g., "The boy has a dog," or "The girls are playing.")				
Independently responds to questions with a sentence including appropriate use of linking verbs				
With prompting and support, responds to a question with a sentence that includes a prepositional or descriptive phrase (e.g., "The monkey is in the tree," or "The shark has lots of teeth.")				
Independently responds to questions with a sentence that includes a prepositional or descriptive phrase				
Appropriately uses a variety of verb tenses in sentences				
Add additional targets				

If your student has not met the prerequisite skills for this standard, drill down to SL.K.6.

Procedure and Data Collection: Run 10–20 trials per session with a **Y** or **N** per trial. Graph the overall percentage of the number correct on the Per Opportunity Graph.

Mastery Criterion: 80% correct across three consecutive sessions with two different instructors.

STRAND
Language

LANGUAGE OVERVIEW

· Understands and uses conventions of English language

· Acquires new vocabulary from a variety of sources and uses it in conversation

CCSS CODE	STANDARD
L.1.1	Demonstrate command of the conventions of standard English grammar and usage when writing or speaking.
L.1.1.a	Print all upper- and lowercase letters.
L.1.1.b	Use common, proper, and possessive nouns.
L.1.1.c	Use singular and plural nouns with matching verbs in basic sentences (e.g., He hops; We hop).
L.1.1.d	Use personal, possessive, and indefinite pronouns (e.g., I, me, my; they, them, their, anyone, everything).
L.1.1.e	Use verbs to convey a sense of past, present, and future (e.g., Yesterday I walked home; Today I walk home; Tomorrow I will walk home).
L.1.1.f	Use frequently occurring adjectives.
L.1.1.g	Use frequently occurring conjunctions (e.g., *and, but, or, so, because*).
L.1.1.h	Use determiners (e.g., articles, demonstratives).
L.1.1.i	Use frequently occurring prepositions (e.g., *during, beyond, toward*).
L.1.1.j	Produce and expand complete simple and compound declarative, interrogative, imperative, and exclamatory sentences in response to prompts.
L.1.2	Demonstrate command of the conventions of standard English capitalization, punctuation, and spelling when writing.
L.1.2.a	Capitalize dates and names of people.
L.1.2.b	Use end punctuation for sentences.
L.1.2.c	Use commas in dates and to separate single words in a series.
L.1.2.d	Use conventional spelling for words with common spelling patterns and for frequently occurring irregular words.
L.1.2.e	Spell untaught words phonetically, drawing on phonemic awareness and spelling conventions.
L.1.3	(L.1.3 begins in grade 2)
L.1.4	Determine or clarify the meaning of unknown and multiple-meaning words and phrases based on *grade 1 reading and content*, choosing flexibly from an array of strategies.
L.1.4.a	Use sentence-level context as a clue to the meaning of a word or phrase.

(continued)

L.1.4.b	Use frequently occurring affixes as a clue to the meaning of a word.
L.1.4.c	Identify frequently occurring root words (e.g., *look*) and their inflectional forms (e.g., *looks, looked, looking*).
L.1.5	With guidance and support from adults, demonstrate understanding of word relationships and nuances in word meanings.
L.1.5.a	Sort words into categories (e.g., colors, clothing) to gain a sense of the concepts the categories represent.
L.1.5.b	Define words by category and by one or more key attributes (e.g., a *duck* is a bird that swims; a *tiger* is a large cat with stripes).
L.1.5.c	Identify real-life connections between words and their use (e.g., note places at home that are *cozy*).
L.1.5.d	Distinguish shades of meaning among verbs differing in manner (e.g., *look, peek, glance, stare, glare, scowl*) and adjectives differing in intensity (e.g., *large, gigantic*) by defining or choosing them or by acting out the meanings.
L.1.6	Use words and phrases acquired through conversations, reading and being read to, and responding to texts, including using frequently occurring conjunctions to signal simple relationships (e.g., *because*).

KIT MATERIALS
- *Writing Prompts Cards*: L.1.1.b, L.1.1.c, L.1.1.d, L.1.1.f, L.1.1.h, L.1.1.j, L.1.2.b
- *Talking in Sentences*: L.1.1.c, L.1.1.d, L.1.1.e, L.1.1.f, L.1.1.i, L.1.4.c, L.1.5.b
- *Speaker's Box*: L.1.1.c, L.1.1.h, L.1.1.j, L.1.2.b
- *Sentence Building Dominoes*: L.1.1.c, L.1.1.d, L.1.1.e, L.1.1.f, L.1.1.g, L.1.1.h, L.1.1.i, L.1.1.j, L.1.2.b, L.1.4.c, L.1.5.a, L.1.5.b
- *SpinZone Magnetic Whiteboard Spinners*: L.1.1.d, L.1.1.e, L.1.1.f, L.1.1.h, L.1.1.i, L.1.2.b, L.1.4.b, L.1.4.c, L.1.5.a, L.1.5.b, L.1.5.d
- *Write-on/Wipe-off Crayons*: L.1.1.d, L.1.1.e, L.1.1.f, L.1.1.i, L.1.2.b, L.1.5.a, L.1.5.d
- *Word Building Cubes*: L.1.2.d, L.1.2.e
- *Big Box of Word Chunks*: L.1.2.d, L.1.2.e, L.1.5.b, L.1.5.c

CLASSROOM MATERIALS AND ACTIVITIES
- Handwriting paper
- Classroom art supplies
- Dictionary
- Sentence strips

TIP FOR GENERALIZATION

Take a community walk. Instruct students to take pictures around the community. Upon returning to the classroom, students each select one picture to write or tell a story about. To meet individual student needs, you can set specific goals such as using prepositions, identifying categories, or writing in the past tense. Students can share their story with a peer.

Language
Conventions of Standard English
**L.1.1: L.1.1.a, L.1.1.b, L.1.1.c, L.1.1.d, L.1.1.e, L.1.1.f,
L.1.1.g, L.1.1.h, L.1.1.i, L.1.1.j
L.1.2: L.1.2.a, L.1.2.b, L.1.2.c, L.1.2.d, L.1.2.e**

L.1.1*

Demonstrate command of the conventions of standard English grammar and usage when writing or speaking.

This standard is divided into ten more specified standards: L.1.1.a, L.1.1.b, L.1.1.c, L.1.1.d, L.1.1.e, L.1.1.f, L.1.1.g, L.1.1.h, L.1.1.i, and L.1.1.j. Once these ten standards have been met, L.1.1 is considered mastered.

L.1.1.a

Print all upper- and lowercase letters.

Materials: Classroom handwriting paper and writing utensils

Teaching Procedure: Provide students with paper and writing utensils. Model writing the letter you expect students to print. Allow them time to practice and provide prompts as needed. For learners who find writing activities aversive, provide individualized highly-motivating materials such as different types of paper or writing utensils unique to this activity.

"Show me a ___." "Write a ___." "What does a ___ look like?"

TARGET	INTRODUCED	MASTERED	GENERALIZATION PROBE	
Traces at least five uppercase letters staying within one centimeter of the line				
Traces at least 10 uppercase letters staying within one centimeter of the line				
Traces all of the uppercase letters staying within one centimeter of the line				
Creates letters by tracing finger in sand or similar texture for at least five uppercase letters				
Creates letters by tracing finger in sand or similar texture for 10 or more uppercase letters				
Independently writes at least five uppercase letters				
Independently writes at least 10 uppercase letters				
Independently writes all uppercase letters				
Independently writes at least five lowercase letters				
Independently writes at least 10 lowercase letters				
Independently writes all lowercase letters				

(continued)

Language
Conventions of Standard English
**L.1.1: L.1.1.a, L.1.1.b, L.1.1.c, L.1.1.d, L.1.1.e, L.1.1.f,
L.1.1.g, L.1.1.h, L.1.1.i, L.1.1.j
L.1.2: L.1.2.a, L.1.2.b, L.1.2.c, L.1.2.d, L.1.2.e**

STUDENT: _____

(L.1.1.a page 2)

Add additional targets				

If your student has not met the prerequisite skills for this standard, drill down to L.K.1.a.

Procedure and Data Collection: Run 10-20 trials per session with a **Y** or **N** per trial.
Graph the overall percentage of the number correct on the Per Opportunity Graph.

Mastery Criterion: 80% correct across three consecutive sessions with two different instructors.

Language
Conventions of Standard English
L.1.1: L.1.1.a, L.1.1.b, L.1.1.c, L.1.1.d, L.1.1.e, L.1.1.f,
L.1.1.g, L.1.1.h, L.1.1.i, L.1.1.j
L.1.2: L.1.2.a, L.1.2.b, L.1.2.c, L.1.2.d, L.1.2.e

STUDENT: _____

L.1.1*

Demonstrate command of the conventions of standard English grammar and usage when writing or speaking.

This standard is divided into ten more specified standards: L.1.1.a, L.1.1.b, L.1.1.c, L.1.1.d, L.1.1.e, L.1.1.f, L.1.1.g, L.1.1.h, L.1.1.i, and L.1.1.j. Once these ten standards have been met, L.1.1 is considered mastered.

L.1.1.b

Use common, proper, and possessive nouns.

Materials: *Writing Prompts Cards*, Classroom reading materials

Teaching Procedure: Prior to teaching the lesson, generate a list of common nouns and a list of proper nouns. Define common and proper nouns for your students. Explain that a common noun begins with a lowercase letter, while a proper noun begins with an uppercase letter. Give several examples of each, then tell them they will play Common/Proper. In this game, students stand up tall (like a capital letter) when they hear a proper noun, and sit in their seat (like a lowercase letter) when they hear a common noun. When introducing possessive nouns, you can do a similar activity.

Then, define a possessive noun, provide several examples, then tell students they will play "Be the Apostrophe." In this game, students read a sentence the teacher has written on the board, then bend their bodies into an apostrophe shape if they see a possessive noun. You can make the game more challenging by including possessive nouns that are missing the apostrophe, then have a student come up and correct the sentence.

"Give me an example of a proper noun." "Should that be capitalized?" "What punctuation mark do I need to show that the ball belongs to the girl?"

TARGET	INTRODUCED	MASTERED	GENERALIZATION PROBE
When asked, states that a common noun is a "person, place, thing, or idea"			
When asked, states that a proper noun is a "specific person, place, or thing"			
Gives at least one example of a proper noun that is a person			
Gives three or more examples of a proper noun that is a person			
Gives at least one example of a proper noun that is a place			
Gives three or more examples of a proper noun that is a place			
Gives at least one example of a proper noun that is a thing			

(continued)

Language
Conventions of Standard English
**L.1.1: L.1.1.a, L.1.1.b, L.1.1.c, L.1.1.d, L.1.1.e, L.1.1.f,
L.1.1.g, L.1.1.h, L.1.1.i, L.1.1.j
L.1.2: L.1.2.a, L.1.2.b, L.1.2.c, L.1.2.d, L.1.2.e**

STUDENT: _____

(L.1.1.b page 2)

Gives three or more examples of a proper noun that is a thing				
When writing, capitalizes the first letter of a proper noun in 80% of opportunities				
When asked, states that a possessive noun "shows ownership"				
When shown a sentence, points to the possessive noun in 80% of opportunities				
When shown a sentence, points to the possessive noun and tells its object in 80% of opportunities				
When writing, correctly uses possessive nouns for singular nouns (by adding an apostrophe "s") in 80% of opportunities				
When writing, correctly uses possessive nouns for plural nouns (by adding an apostrophe after the "s") in 80% of opportunities				
Add additional targets				

  If your student has not met the prerequisite skills for this standard, drill down to L.K.1.b.

  Procedure and Data Collection: Run 10-20 trials per session with a **Y** or **N** per trial. Graph the overall percentage of the number correct on the Per Opportunity Graph.

Mastery Criterion: 80% correct across three consecutive sessions with two different instructors.

Language
Conventions of Standard English
**L.1.1: L.1.1.a, L.1.1.b, L.1.1.c, L.1.1.d, L.1.1.e, L.1.1.f,
L.1.1.g, L.1.1.h, L.1.1.i, L.1.1.j
L.1.2: L.1.2.a, L.1.2.b, L.1.2.c, L.1.2.d, L.1.2.e**

STUDENT: _____

L.1.1*

Demonstrate command of the conventions of standard English grammar and usage when writing or speaking.

This standard is divided into ten more specified standards: L.1.1.a, L.1.1.b, L.1.1.c, L.1.1.d, L.1.1.e, L.1.1.f, L.1.1.g, L.1.1.h, L.1.1.i, and L.1.1.j. Once these ten standards have been met, L.1.1 is considered mastered.

L.1.1.c

Use singular and plural nouns with matching verbs in basic sentences (e.g., He hops; We hop).

Materials: *Sentence Building Dominoes, Talking in Sentences (pages 26–29), Speaker's Box, Writing Prompts Cards*

Teaching Procedure: Prior to the lesson, remove several nouns and verbs from the *Sentence Building Dominoes* container. Also remove the two tiles that show "s" and "es." Explain that in sentences, subjects and verbs must match, and that "opposites attract." A singular verb ends in "-s" or "-es," while a plural verb does not (which is the opposite of singular and plural nouns). List several examples, such as "The dogs play" and "The baby laughs." Have students find the noun, identify the noun as singular or plural, then find the verb and identify it as singular or plural. Then, place the *Sentence Building Dominoes* you've removed prior to the lesson on the table. Build short sentences, then have students take turns either labeling the verb as "matching" or adding an "-s" or "-es" to the verb to make it match the noun. If your students are not yet familiar with rules related to adding "-es" just choose verbs that can be pluralized by adding an "-s."

"Does this verb match the subject?" "Should we add an '-s' here?" "How can we fix this sentence?"

TARGET	INTRODUCED	MASTERED	GENERALIZATION PROBE	
When asked how to make a word plural, responds "add an '-s'"				
Adds an "-s" to verbs when the subject noun is singular in 80% of opportunities				
When asked how to make a word that ends in "-ch" or "-sh" (such as "wash" or "catch") plural, responds "add an '-es'"				
When asked how to make a word that ends in "-x" or "-s" (such as "box" or "mess") plural, responds "add an '-es'"				
When presented with several sentences, some written correctly, others with verbs that do not match the subject noun, corrects sentences appropriately in 80% of opportunities				
When speaking, uses matching verbs correctly in 80% of opportunities				
When writing, uses matching verbs correctly in 80% of opportunities				

(continued)

Language
Conventions of Standard English
**L.1.1: L.1.1.a, L.1.1.b, L.1.1.c, L.1.1.d, L.1.1.e, L.1.1.f,
L.1.1.g, L.1.1.h, L.1.1.i, L.1.1.j
L.1.2: L.1.2.a, L.1.2.b, L.1.2.c, L.1.2.d, L.1.2.e**

STUDENT: _____

(L.1.1.c page 2)

Add additional targets				

If your student has not met the prerequisite skills for this standard, drill down to L.K.1.c.

Procedure and Data Collection: Run 10-20 trials per session with a **Y** or **N** per trial.
Graph the overall percentage of the number correct on the Per Opportunity Graph.

Mastery Criterion: 80% correct across three consecutive sessions with two different instructors.

Language
Conventions of Standard English
L.1.1: L.1.1.a, L.1.1.b, L.1.1.c, L.1.1.d, L.1.1.e, L.1.1.f,
L.1.1.g, L.1.1.h, L.1.1.i, L.1.1.j
L.1.2: L.1.2.a, L.1.2.b, L.1.2.c, L.1.2.d, L.1.2.e

L.1.1*

Demonstrate command of the conventions of standard English grammar and usage when writing or speaking.

This standard is divided into ten more specified standards: L.1.1.a, L.1.1.b, L.1.1.c, L.1.1.d, L.1.1.e, L.1.1.f, L.1.1.g, L.1.1.h, L.1.1.i, and L.1.1.j. Once these ten standards have been met, L.1.1 is considered mastered.

L.1.1.d

Use personal, possessive, and indefinite pronouns (e.g., I, me, my; they, them, their, anyone, everything).

Materials: *Talking in Sentences (pages 8 – 13), SpinZone Magnetic Whiteboard Spinners, Sentence Building Dominoes, Writing Prompts Cards, Write-on/Wipe-off Crayons*

Teaching Procedure: Prior to the lesson about personal pronouns, read through that day's lesson in *Talking in Sentences*. Place the book flat on the table so you can easily read the text on page 9 while the picture on page 8 is in full view of your students. Read the introduction, then take your students through the Listen and Respond, Talk About, and Let's Talk sections of the lesson. You can also create specific questions in advance to use with pictures of your student's favorite people, places and things if your student struggles with this skill.

Prior to introducing possessive pronouns, students must have mastered possessive nouns. After introducing possessive pronouns, you can use the *SpinZone Magnetic Whiteboard Spinners* to practice using them correctly. Attach a spinner to the whiteboard, draw a circle around it, and then divide it into the necessary number of parts for your lesson. For example, if you are focusing on all possessive pronouns, you might divide the circle into six parts, then write a pronoun in each section (e.g., mine, yours, his, hers, ours, and theirs). Students take turns spinning the spinner, and then using the word correctly in a sentence. The same activity can be used to practice indefinite pronouns, or practice using all three types of pronouns addressed in this standard simultaneously.

"Look at the picture. Whose shirt is red?" "That toy belongs to the girl. The toy is ___."

TARGET	INTRODUCED	MASTERED	GENERALIZATION PROBE	
When speaking, uses "I" and "me" appropriately in 80% of opportunities				
When writing, uses "I" and "me" appropriately in 80% of opportunities				
When speaking, uses "he," "she," and "it" appropriately in 80% of opportunities				
When writing, uses "he," "she," and "it" appropriately in 80% of opportunities				
When speaking, uses "we" and "they" appropriately in 80% of opportunities				
When writing, uses "we" and "they" appropriately in 80% of opportunities				

(continued)

Language
Conventions of Standard English
**L.1.1: L.1.1.a, L.1.1.b, L.1.1.c, L.1.1.d, L.1.1.e, L.1.1.f,
L.1.1.g, L.1.1.h, L.1.1.i, L.1.1.j
L.1.2: L.1.2.a, L.1.2.b, L.1.2.c, L.1.2.d, L.1.2.e**

STUDENT: _____

(L.1.1.d page 2)

When speaking, uses "mine" and "yours" appropriately in 80% of opportunities				
When writing, uses "mine" and "yours" appropriately in 80% of opportunities				
When speaking, uses "his" and "hers" appropriately in 80% of opportunities				
When writing, uses "his" and "hers" appropriately in 80% of opportunities				
When speaking, uses "ours" and "theirs" appropriately in 80% of opportunities				
When writing, uses "ours" and "theirs" appropriately in 80% of opportunities				
When speaking, uses at least three indefinite pronouns (such as anyone, everyone, or something) appropriately in 80% of opportunities				
When writing, uses at least three indefinite pronouns appropriately in 80% of opportunities				
When speaking, uses five or more indefinite pronouns appropriately in 80% of opportunities				
When writing, uses five or more indefinite pronouns appropriately in 80% of opportunities				
Add additional targets				

⚠ **If your student has not met the prerequisite skills for this standard, drill down to L.K.1.b, L.K.1.c.**

Procedure and Data Collection: Run 10-20 trials per session with a **Y** or **N** per trial. Graph the overall percentage of the number correct on the Per Opportunity Graph.

Mastery Criterion: 80% correct across three consecutive sessions with two different instructors.

Language
Conventions of Standard English
**L.1.1: L.1.1.a, L.1.1.b, L.1.1.c, L.1.1.d, L.1.1.e, L.1.1.f,
L.1.1.g, L.1.1.h, L.1.1.i, L.1.1.j
L.1.2: L.1.2.a, L.1.2.b, L.1.2.c, L.1.2.d, L.1.2.e**

STUDENT: _____

L.1.1*

Demonstrate command of the conventions of standard English grammar and usage when writing or speaking.

This standard is divided into ten more specified standards: L.1.1.a, L.1.1.b, L.1.1.c, L.1.1.d, L.1.1.e, L.1.1.f, L.1.1.g, L.1.1.h, L.1.1.i, and L.1.1.j. Once these ten standards have been met, L.1.1 is considered mastered.

L.1.1.e

Use verbs to convey a sense of past, present, and future (e.g., Yesterday I walked home; Today I walk home; Tomorrow I will walk home).

 Materials: *SpinZone Magnetic Whiteboard Spinners, Write-on/Wipe-off Crayons, Talking in Sentences, Sentence Building Dominoes*

 Teaching Procedure: Attach a spinner to the whiteboard, draw a circle around it, and then divide it into three parts. Label the parts "past," "present," and "future." Say a word, such as "walk." Students take turns spinning the spinner and changing the word to the correct tense. To make the activity simpler, add textual cues in each part of the circle (such as putting "-ed" under the word "past".) To make it more challenging, say a complete sentence, and then have each student use the new verb in a complete sentence after spinning.

 "Today I jump, yesterday I _____." "Can you fix the sentence?"

TARGET	INTRODUCED	MASTERED	GENERALIZATION PROBE
When speaking, uses past tense verbs appropriately in 80% of opportunities			
When writing, uses past tense verbs appropriately in 80% of opportunities			
When speaking, uses present tense verbs appropriately in 80% of opportunities			
When writing, uses present tense verbs appropriately in 80% of opportunities			
When speaking, uses future tense verbs appropriately in 80% of opportunities			
When writing, uses future tense verbs appropriately in 80% of opportunities			
When presented with several sentences, some written correctly, others with verbs in the wrong tense, corrects sentences appropriately in 80% of opportunities			

(continued)

Language
Conventions of Standard English
**L.1.1: L.1.1.a, L.1.1.b, L.1.1.c, L.1.1.d, L.1.1.e, L.1.1.f,
L.1.1.g, L.1.1.h, L.1.1.i, L.1.1.j
L.1.2: L.1.2.a, L.1.2.b, L.1.2.c, L.1.2.d, L.1.2.e**

STUDENT: _____

(L.1.1.e page 2)

Add additional targets				

 If your student has not met the prerequisite skills for this standard, drill down to L.K.1.b.

 Procedure and Data Collection: Run 10–20 trials per session with a **Y** or **N** per trial.
Graph the overall percentage of the number correct on the Per Opportunity Graph.

Mastery Criterion: 80% correct across three consecutive sessions with two different instructors.

Language
Conventions of Standard English
**L.1.1: L.1.1.a, L.1.1.b, L.1.1.c, L.1.1.d, L.1.1.e, L.1.1.f,
L.1.1.g, L.1.1.h, L.1.1.i, L.1.1.j
L.1.2: L.1.2.a, L.1.2.b, L.1.2.c, L.1.2.d, L.1.2.e**

L.1.1*

Demonstrate command of the conventions of standard English grammar and usage when writing or speaking.

This standard is divided into ten more specified standards: L.1.1.a, L.1.1.b, L.1.1.c, L.1.1.d, L.1.1.e, L.1.1.f, L.1.1.g, L.1.1.h, L.1.1.i, and L.1.1.j. Once these ten standards have been met, L.1.1 is considered mastered.

L.1.1.f

Use frequently occurring adjectives.

Materials: *SpinZone Magnetic Whiteboard Spinners, Write-on/Wipe-off Crayons, Sentence Building Dominoes, Talking in Sentences, Writing Prompts Cards*

Teaching Procedure: Attach a spinner to the whiteboard, draw a circle around it, and then divide it into the appropriate number of parts for your lesson. For example, if your students have already mastered the use of four adjectives, and you are introducing two new ones, separate the circle into six parts. Write an adjective in each section. Students take turns spinning the spinner, then defining and/or using the adjective in a sentence.

"Describe the boy." "Which ball did you want?"

TARGET	INTRODUCED	MASTERED	GENERALIZATION PROBE	
When provided with an adjective related to color, points to a picture or object that is described by that adjective				
When provided with an adjective related to size (e.g., tall, short, long), points to a picture or object that is described by that adjective				
When provided with an adjective related to touch (e.g., sticky, slippery), points to a picture or object that is described by that adjective				
When provided with an adjective related to feelings (e.g., happy, sad), points to a picture or object that is described by that adjective				
When provided with an adjective related to qualities (e.g., good, silly, new), points to a picture or object that is described by that adjective				
Uses at least two adjectives to describe pictures and objects				
Uses at least five adjectives to describe pictures and objects				
Consistently uses 10 or more adjectives to describe pictures and objects				

(continued)

Language
Conventions of Standard English
**L.1.1: L.1.1.a, L.1.1.b, L.1.1.c, L.1.1.d, L.1.1.e, L.1.1.f,
L.1.1.g, L.1.1.h, L.1.1.i, L.1.1.j
L.1.2: L.1.2.a, L.1.2.b, L.1.2.c, L.1.2.d, L.1.2.e**

STUDENT: _____

(L.1.1.f page 2)

Add additional targets				

 If your student has not met the prerequisite skills for this standard, drill down to L.K.1.b.

 Procedure and Data Collection: Run 10–20 trials per session with a **Y** or **N** per trial.
Graph the overall percentage of the number correct on the Per Opportunity Graph.

Mastery Criterion: 80% correct across three consecutive sessions with two different instructors.

Language
Conventions of Standard English
L.1.1: L.1.1.a, L.1.1.b, L.1.1.c, L.1.1.d, L.1.1.e, L.1.1.f, L.1.1.g, L.1.1.h, L.1.1.i, L.1.1.j
L.1.2: L.1.2.a, L.1.2.b, L.1.2.c, L.1.2.d, L.1.2.e

L.1.1*

Demonstrate command of the conventions of standard English grammar and usage when writing or speaking.

This standard is divided into ten more specified standards: L.1.1.a, L.1.1.b, L.1.1.c, L.1.1.d, L.1.1.e, L.1.1.f, L.1.1.g, L.1.1.h, L.1.1.i, and L.1.1.j. Once these ten standards have been met, L.1.1 is considered mastered.

L.1.1.g

Use frequently occurring conjunctions (e.g., *and, but, or, so, because*).

Materials: *Sentence Building Dominoes*

Teaching Procedure: Prior to the lesson, prepare sentences using the *Sentence Building Dominoes*. Set aside the tiles for *and, but, or, so*, and *because*. Depending on your students' abilities, you may want to introduce only one conjunction at a time. Using the *Sentence Building Dominoes*, model for students how you would combine two sentences using a conjunction. Then give students sets of sentences and have them combine the sentences using a conjunction.

"How can we combine these two sentences?" "Can you put these two sentences together?" "What word would you use?"

TARGET	INTRODUCED	MASTERED	GENERALIZATION PROBE	
When provided with two sentences, uses the word *and* to combine them				
When provided with two sentences, uses the word *but* to combine them				
When provided with two sentences, uses the word *because* to combine them				
When provided with two sentences, uses the word *or* to combine them				
When provided with two sentences, uses the word *so* to combine them				
Appropriately uses the word *and* to combine sentences in conversation				
Appropriately uses the word *but* to combine sentences in conversation				
Appropriately uses the word *because* to combine sentences in conversation				
Appropriately uses the word *or* to combine sentences in conversation				
Appropriately uses the word *so* to combine sentences in conversation				

(continued)

Language
Conventions of Standard English
**L.1.1: L.1.1.a, L.1.1.b, L.1.1.c, L.1.1.d, L.1.1.e, L.1.1.f,
L.1.1.g, L.1.1.h, L.1.1.i, L.1.1.j
L.1.2: L.1.2.a, L.1.2.b, L.1.2.c, L.1.2.d, L.1.2.e**

STUDENT: _____

(L.1.1.g page 2)

Add additional targets				

⚠ **If your student has not met the prerequisite skills for this standard, drill down to L.K.1.b, L.K.1.f.**

Procedure and Data Collection: Run 10–20 trials per session with a **Y** or **N** per trial.
Graph the overall percentage of the number correct on the Per Opportunity Graph.

Mastery Criterion: 80% correct across three consecutive sessions with two different instructors.

STUDENT: _____

Language
Conventions of Standard English
**L.1.1: L.1.1.a, L.1.1.b, L.1.1.c, L.1.1.d, L.1.1.e, L.1.1.f,
L.1.1.g, L.1.1.h, L.1.1.i, L.1.1.j
L.1.2: L.1.2.a, L.1.2.b, L.1.2.c, L.1.2.d, L.1.2.e**

L.1.1*

Demonstrate command of the conventions of standard English grammar and usage when writing or speaking.

This standard is divided into ten more specified standards: L.1.1.a, L.1.1.b, L.1.1.c, L.1.1.d, L.1.1.e, L.1.1.f, L.1.1.g, L.1.1.h, L.1.1.i, and L.1.1.j. Once these ten standards have been met, L.1.1 is considered mastered.

L.1.1.h

Use determiners (e.g., articles, demonstratives).

Materials: *Speaker's Box, Sentence Building Dominoes, SpinZone Magnetic Whiteboard Spinners, Writing Prompts Cards*

Teaching Procedure: Use the black "What's Happening Here?/What Comes Next?" or the blue "Things You Like Best" cards from the *Speaker's Box*. Present a card for discussion. During the discussion, ask questions to provide opportunities for each student to use their target word. For example, if your student's goal is to use demonstratives, you might point to the picture and ask, "Which eggs did he break?" in order for the student to respond "*Those* eggs."

Note: If your student is not able to meet any of the prerequisite skills for this standard, you should assess using the VB-MAPP and start with developmentally appropriate goals.

"Tell me more." "To whom do the shoes belong?" "Write a complete sentence."

TARGET	INTRODUCED	MASTERED	GENERALIZATION PROBE	
When speaking, uses articles (i.e., *a, an, the*) appropriately in 80% of opportunities				
When writing, uses articles appropriately in 80% of opportunities				
When speaking, uses demonstratives (i.e., *this, that, these*) appropriately in 80% of opportunities				
When writing, uses demonstratives appropriately in 80% of opportunities				
When speaking, uses possessive determiners (i.e., *my, your, his*) appropriately in 80% of opportunities				
When writing, uses possessive determiners appropriately in 80% of opportunities				
When speaking, uses interrogatives (i.e., *which, what*) appropriately in 80% of opportunities				
When writing, uses interrogatives appropriately in 80% of opportunities				
When speaking, uses quantifiers (i.e., *many, few, several*) appropriately in 80% of opportunities				
When writing, uses quantifiers appropriately in 80% of opportunities				

(continued)

Language
Conventions of Standard English
L.1.1: L.1.1.a, L.1.1.b, L.1.1.c, L.1.1.d, L.1.1.e, L.1.1.f, L.1.1.g, L.1.1.h, L.1.1.i, L.1.1.j
L.1.2: L.1.2.a, L.1.2.b, L.1.2.c, L.1.2.d, L.1.2.e

STUDENT: _____

(L.1.1.h page 2)

Add additional targets				

⚠ **If your student has not met the prerequisite skills for this standard, drill down to L.K.1.b, L.K.1.f.**

Procedure and Data Collection: Run 10–20 trials per session with a **Y** or **N** per trial. Graph the overall percentage of the number correct on the Per Opportunity Graph.

Mastery Criterion: 80% correct across three consecutive sessions with two different instructors.

Language
Conventions of Standard English
**L.1.1: L.1.1.a, L.1.1.b, L.1.1.c, L.1.1.d, L.1.1.e, L.1.1.f,
L.1.1.g, L.1.1.h, L.1.1.i, L.1.1.j
L.1.2: L.1.2.a, L.1.2.b, L.1.2.c, L.1.2.d, L.1.2.e**

L.1.1*

Demonstrate command of the conventions of standard English grammar and usage when writing or speaking.

This standard is divided into ten more specified standards: L.1.1.a, L.1.1.b, L.1.1.c, L.1.1.d, L.1.1.e, L.1.1.f, L.1.1.g, L.1.1.h, L.1.1.i, and L.1.1.j. Once these ten standards have been met, L.1.1 is considered mastered.

L.1.1.i

Use frequently occurring prepositions (e.g., *during, beyond, toward*).

Materials: *Talking in Sentences (pages 42 – 43), SpinZone Magnetic Whiteboard Spinners,* Write-on/ *Wipe-off Crayons, Sentence Building Dominoes*

Teaching Procedure: Prior to the lesson about prepositions, read through that day's lesson in *Talking in Sentences*. Place the book flat on the table so you can easily read the text on page 43 while the picture on page 42 is in full view of your students. Read the introduction, then take your students through the Listen and Respond, Talk About, and Let's Talk sections of the lesson. For students who struggle with using prepositions, you may need to introduce three or fewer prepositions at a time and provide 3D examples, such as using a cup and placing a block *under* the cup, then placing it *in* the cup. For active practice of prepositions, you can place a *SpinZone Magnetic Whiteboard Spinner* on the board, draw a circle around it, and divide the circle into the appropriate number of spaces with a preposition in each space. Students take turns spinning the spinner and then demonstrating the preposition (e.g., putting a block *on* their head or squatting *under* a desk).

"Which girl is standing next to the ball?" "Can you draw a ball under the table?" "Where is the chalk?"

TARGET	INTRODUCED	MASTERED	GENERALIZATION PROBE
When speaking, uses at least one preposition appropriately in 80% of opportunities			
When writing, uses at least one preposition appropriately in 80% of opportunities			
When speaking, uses three or more prepositions appropriately in 80% of opportunities			
When writing, uses three or more prepositions appropriately in 80% of opportunities			
When speaking, uses five or more prepositions appropriately in 80% of opportunities			
When writing, uses five or more prepositions appropriately in 80% of opportunities			
When speaking, uses 10 or more prepositions appropriately in 80% of opportunities			
When writing, uses 10 or more prepositions appropriately in 80% of opportunities			

(continued)

Language
Conventions of Standard English
L.1.1: L.1.1.a, L.1.1.b, L.1.1.c, L.1.1.d, L.1.1.e, L.1.1.f, L.1.1.g, L.1.1.h, L.1.1.i, L.1.1.j
L.1.2: L.1.2.a, L.1.2.b, L.1.2.c, L.1.2.d, L.1.2.e

STUDENT: _____

(L.1.1.i page 2)

Add additional targets				

 If your student has not met the prerequisite skills for this standard, drill down to L.K.1.e.

 Procedure and Data Collection: Run 10–20 trials per session with a **Y** or **N** per trial. Graph the overall percentage of the number correct on the Per Opportunity Graph.

Mastery Criterion: 80% correct across three consecutive sessions with two different instructors.

Language
Conventions of Standard English
**L.1.1: L.1.1.a, L.1.1.b, L.1.1.c, L.1.1.d, L.1.1.e, L.1.1.f,
L.1.1.g, L.1.1.h, L.1.1.i, L.1.1.j
L.1.2: L.1.2.a, L.1.2.b, L.1.2.c, L.1.2.d, L.1.2.e**

L.1.1*

Demonstrate command of the conventions of standard English grammar and usage when writing or speaking.

*This standard is divided into ten more specified standards: L.1.1.a, L.1.1.b, L.1.1.c, L.1.1.d, L.1.1.e, L.1.1.f, L.1.1.g, L.1.1.h, L.1.1.i, and L.1.1.j. Once these ten standards have been met, L.1.1 is considered mastered.

L.1.1.j

Produce and expand complete simple and compound declarative, interrogative, imperative, and exclamatory sentences in response to prompts.

Materials: *Speaker's Box, Sentence Building Dominoes, Writing Prompts Cards*

Teaching Procedure: Use the *Speaker's Box* and select cards that match your students' interest areas. Present a card for discussion. During the discussion, provide opportunities for students to produce sentences. Then, provide prompts as necessary to help them expand those sentences.

Note: If your student is not able to meet any of the prerequisite skills for this standard, you should assess using the VB-MAPP and start with developmentally appropriate goals.

"Tell me more." "Can you connect those two sentences using the word 'but?'"

TARGET	INTRODUCED	MASTERED	GENERALIZATION PROBE	
With prompting and support, responds to a question with a simple declarative sentence (e.g., "The girl jumped.")				
Independently responds to questions with a simple declarative sentence				
With prompting and support, writes a simple declarative sentence				
Independently writes a simple declarative sentence				
With prompting and support, responds to a question with a simple interrogative sentence (e.g., "Why did the girl jump?")				
Independently responds to questions with a simple interrogative sentence				
With prompting and support, writes a simple interrogative sentence				
Independently writes a simple interrogative sentence				
With prompting and support, responds to a question with a simple imperative sentence (e.g., "Clean your room now.")				
Independently responds to questions with a simple imperative sentence				

(continued)

Language
Conventions of Standard English
**L.1.1: L.1.1.a, L.1.1.b, L.1.1.c, L.1.1.d, L.1.1.e, L.1.1.f,
L.1.1.g, L.1.1.h, L.1.1.i, L.1.1.j
L.1.2: L.1.2.a, L.1.2.b, L.1.2.c, L.1.2.d, L.1.2.e**

STUDENT: _____

(L.1.1.j page 2)

With prompting and support, writes a simple imperative sentence				
Independently writes a simple imperative sentence				
With prompting and support, responds to a question with a simple exclamatory sentence (e.g., "Run fast!")				
Independently responds to questions with a simple exclamatory sentence				
With prompting and support, writes a simple exclamatory sentence				
Independently writes a simple exclamatory sentence				
With prompting and support, uses a conjunction to create a compound sentence				
Independently uses a conjunction to create a compound sentence				
With prompting and support, adds details or information to expand a sentence				
Independently adds details or information to expand a sentence				
Add additional targets				

If your student has not met the prerequisite skills for this standard, drill down to L.K.1.f.

Procedure and Data Collection: Run 10–20 trials per session with a **Y** or **N** per trial. Graph the overall percentage of the number correct on the Per Opportunity Graph.

Mastery Criterion: 80% correct across three consecutive sessions with two different instructors.

STUDENT: _____

Language
Conventions of Standard English
**L.1.1: L.1.1.a, L.1.1.b, L.1.1.c, L.1.1.d, L.1.1.e, L.1.1.f,
L.1.1.g, L.1.1.h, L.1.1.i, L.1.1.j
L.1.2: L.1.2.a, L.1.2.b, L.1.2.c, L.1.2.d, L.1.2.e**

L.1.2*

Demonstrate command of the conventions of standard English capitalization, punctuation, and spelling when writing.

This standard is divided into five more specified standards: L.1.2.a, L.1.2.b, L.1.2.c, L.1.2.d, and L.1.2.e. Once these five standards have been met, L.1.2 is considered mastered.

L.1.2.a

Capitalize dates and names of people.

Materials: Index cards, Paper (not included in kit)

Teaching Procedure: Prior to the lesson, write several names of months, days of the week, and people on index cards. For each date or name, you will create two index cards, one on which the date or name is capitalized, and one on which it is not. Teach students the convention for the lesson, i.e., "You always capitalize the day of the week." Then, present two index cards, one with "Tuesday" capitalized and one without capitalization. Ask students to point to the index card that is correct. Present several pairs in this fashion to provide practice.

"Which one is correct?" "Do we capitalize the word 'June?'" "What word needs to be capitalized?"

TARGET	INTRODUCED	MASTERED	GENERALIZATION PROBE	
Demonstrates knowledge of the rule "Capitalize all days of the week."				
When presented with a sentence in which a day of the week is not capitalized, states that the word should be capitalized				
When writing, capitalizes all days of the week in 80% of opportunities				
Demonstrates knowledge of the rule "Capitalize all names of months."				
When presented with a sentence in which a month is not capitalized, states that the word should be capitalized				
When writing, capitalizes all months in 80% of opportunities				
Demonstrates knowledge of the rule "Capitalize all names of people."				
When presented with a sentence in which the name of a person is not capitalized, states that the word should be capitalized				
When writing, capitalizes all names of people in 80% of opportunities				

(continued)

Language
Conventions of Standard English
L.1.1: L.1.1.a, L.1.1.b, L.1.1.c, L.1.1.d, L.1.1.e, L.1.1.f,
L.1.1.g, L.1.1.h, L.1.1.i, L.1.1.j
L.1.2: L.1.2.a, L.1.2.b, L.1.2.c, L.1.2.d, L.1.2.e

STUDENT: _____

(L.1.2.a page 2)

Add additional targets				

⚠ **If your student has not met the prerequisite skills for this standard, drill down to L.K.2.a.**

Procedure and Data Collection: Run 10–20 trials per session with a **Y** or **N** per trial.
Graph the overall percentage of the number correct on the Per Opportunity Graph.

Mastery Criterion: 80% correct across three consecutive sessions with two different instructors.

Language
Conventions of Standard English
L.1.1: L.1.1.a, L.1.1.b, L.1.1.c, L.1.1.d, L.1.1.e, L.1.1.f,
L.1.1.g, L.1.1.h, L.1.1.i, L.1.1.j
L.1.2: L.1.2.a, L.1.2.b, L.1.2.c, L.1.2.d, L.1.2.e

L.1.2*

Demonstrate command of the conventions of standard English capitalization, punctuation, and spelling when writing.

This standard is divided into five more specified standards: L.1.2.a, L.1.2.b, L.1.2.c, L.1.2.d, and L.1.2.e. Once these five standards have been met, L.1.2 is considered mastered.

L.1.2.b

Use end punctuation for sentences.

Materials: *SpinZone Magnetic Whiteboard Spinners, Write-on/Wipe-off Crayons, Sentence Building Dominoes, Speaker's Box, Writing Prompts Cards*

Teaching Procedure: Attach a spinner to the whiteboard. Draw a circle around it and then divide it into three parts and write a punctuation mark in each section. Students take turns spinning the spinner, then speaking a sentence that uses that form of end punctuation. For example, if the spinner lands on a question mark, the student might say, "Where are my socks?"

"What punctuation mark should you use for a sentence that starts with the word 'Where?'" "What goes here?" "Should you use a period or an exclamation point here?"

TARGET	INTRODUCED	MASTERED	GENERALIZATION PROBE	
When writing, uses a period at the end of declarative and imperative sentences in 80% of opportunities				
When writing, uses a question mark at the end of interrogative sentences in 80% of opportunities				
When writing, uses an exclamation point at the end of exclamatory sentences in 80% of opportunities				
Add additional targets				

If your student has not met the prerequisite skills for this standard, drill down to L.K.2.b.

Procedure and Data Collection: Run 10–20 trials per session with a **Y** or **N** per trial. Graph the overall percentage of the number correct on the Per Opportunity Graph.

Mastery Criterion: 80% correct across three consecutive sessions with two different instructors.

Language
Conventions of Standard English
L.1.1: L.1.1.a, L.1.1.b, L.1.1.c, L.1.1.d, L.1.1.e, L.1.1.f,
L.1.1.g, L.1.1.h, L.1.1.i, L.1.1.j
L.1.2: L.1.2.a, L.1.2.b, L.1.2.c, L.1.2.d, L.1.2.e

STUDENT: _____

L.1.2* Demonstrate command of the conventions of standard English capitalization, punctuation, and spelling when writing.

*This standard is divided into five more specified standards: L.1.2.a, L.1.2.b, L.1.2.c, L.1.2.d, and L.1.2.e. Once these five standards have been met, L.1.2 is considered mastered.

L.1.2.c Use commas in dates and to separate single words in a series.

 Materials: Sentence strips, Macaroni, Glue (not included in kit)

 Teaching Procedure: Prior to the lesson, write several examples of dates on sentence strips but leave out the commas (e.g., June 26 2008). Explain the rule of placing a comma between the day and the year when writing the date. Provide several examples without the comma on the whiteboard. Give each student one or more sentence strips, pieces of dry macaroni, and glue. Students should glue the macaroni in the spot where a comma belongs.

 "Where does a comma belong?" "What is missing in this sentence?"

TARGET	INTRODUCED	MASTERED	GENERALIZATION PROBE	
With prompting and support, places a comma correctly in a date in 80% of opportunities				
Independently places a comma correctly in a date in 80% of opportunities				
With prompting and support, places commas to separate single words in a series in 80% of opportunities				
Independently places commas to separate single words in a series in 80% of opportunities				
Add additional targets				

 If your student has not met the prerequisite skills for this standard, drill down to L.K.2.b.

 Procedure and Data Collection: Run 10–20 trials per session with a **Y** or **N** per trial. Graph the overall percentage of the number correct on the Per Opportunity Graph.

Mastery Criterion: 80% correct across three consecutive sessions with two different instructors.

Language
Conventions of Standard English
L.1.1: L.1.1.a, L.1.1.b, L.1.1.c, L.1.1.d, L.1.1.e, L.1.1.f, L.1.1.g, L.1.1.h, L.1.1.i, L.1.1.j
L.1.2: L.1.2.a, L.1.2.b, L.1.2.c, L.1.2.d, L.1.2.e

L.1.2* Demonstrate command of the conventions of standard English capitalization, punctuation, and spelling when writing.

*This standard is divided into five more specified standards: L.1.2.a, L.1.2.b, L.1.2.c, L.1.2.d, and L.1.2.e. Once these five standards have been met, L.1.2 is considered mastered.

L.1.2.d Use conventional spelling for words with common spelling patterns and for frequently occurring irregular words.

Materials: *Word Building Cubes, Big Box of Word Chunks*

Teaching Procedure: Prior to the lesson, prepare word lists for each student based on his/her current skill level. Place several *Word Building Cubes* in front of each student (make sure that the cubes contain the letters needed to spell the words you provide). Say a word and have the students use the cubes to spell the word correctly.

"How do you spell ___?" "Sound it out and try again."

TARGET	INTRODUCED	MASTERED	GENERALIZATION PROBE
Spells 25 or more CVC words correctly in 80% of opportunities			
Spells any novel CVC word correctly in 80% of opportunities			
Spells 10 or more frequently occurring irregular words correctly in 80% of opportunities			
Spells 25 or more frequently occurring irregular words correctly in 80% of opportunities			
Spells 10 or more conventional words with common spelling patterns (such as *late, door,* or *pail*) correctly in 80% of opportunities			
Spells 25 or more conventional words with common spelling patterns correctly in 80% of opportunities			
Add additional targets			

If your student has not met the prerequisite skills for this standard, drill down to L.K.2.c, L.K.2.d.

Procedure and Data Collection: Run 10–20 trials per session with a **Y** or **N** per trial. Graph the overall percentage of the number correct on the Per Opportunity Graph.

Mastery Criterion: 80% correct across three consecutive sessions with two different instructors.

Language
Conventions of Standard English
L.1.1: L.1.1.a, L.1.1.b, L.1.1.c, L.1.1.d, L.1.1.e, L.1.1.f,
L.1.1.g, L.1.1.h, L.1.1.i, L.1.1.j
L.1.2: L.1.2.a, L.1.2.b, L.1.2.c, L.1.2.d, L.1.2.e

STUDENT: _____

L.1.2*

Demonstrate command of the conventions of standard English capitalization, punctuation, and spelling when writing.

This standard is divided into five more specified standards: L.1.2.a, L.1.2.b, L.1.2.c, L.1.2.d, and L.1.2.e. Once these five standards have been met, L.1.2 is considered mastered.

L.1.2.e

Spell untaught words phonetically, drawing on phonemic awareness and spelling conventions.

Materials: *Big Box of Word Chunks, Word Building Cubes*

Teaching Procedure: Prior to the lesson, prepare word lists for each student based on his/her current skill level. Place several puzzle pieces from the *Big Box of Word Chunks* on the table within view of the students. Name a word and have students try to find the pieces that spell that word. Once the correct spelling has been found, have all students spell it out loud in unison.

"What letter makes that sound?" "What letter do you think comes next?"

TARGET	INTRODUCED	MASTERED	GENERALIZATION PROBE	
Upon hearing a novel word, is able to identify the first letter accurately in 80% of opportunities				
Upon hearing a novel word, is able to identify the first and last letter accurately in 80% of opportunities				
Upon hearing a novel CVC word, is able to separate the sounds that make up the word and spell it out phonetically in 80% of opportunities				
Upon hearing any novel single-syllable word, is able to separate the sounds and consider phonemic knowledge to spell it out phonetically in 80% of opportunities				
Upon hearing any novel two-syllable word, is able to separate the sounds and utilize phonemic knowledge to spell it out phonetically in 80% of opportunities				
Add additional targets				

If your student has not met the prerequisite skills for this standard, drill down to L.K.2.c, L.K.2.d.

Procedure and Data Collection: Run 10–20 trials per session with a **Y** or **N** per trial. Graph the overall percentage of the number correct on the Per Opportunity Graph.

Mastery Criterion: 80% correct across three consecutive sessions with two different instructors.

STUDENT: _____

> **Language**
> Vocabulary Acquisition and Use
> **L.1.4: L.1.4.a, L.1.4.b, L.1.4.c**
> **L.1.5: L.1.5.a, L.1.5.b, L.1.5.c, L.1.5.d**
> **L.1.6**

L.1.4*

Determine or clarify the meaning of unknown and multiple-meaning words and phrases based on *grade 1 reading and content*, choosing flexibly from an array of strategies.

*This standard is divided into three more specified standards: L.1.4.a, L.1.4.b, and L.1.4.c.
Once these three standards have been met, L.1.4 is considered mastered.

L.1.4.a

Use sentence-level context as a clue to the meaning of a word or phrase.

Materials: Classroom reading materials, Sentence strips, Index Cards (not included in kit)

Teaching Procedure: Prior to the lesson, prepare several sentences on sentence strips that contain unknown words. For each sentence, write answer choices for what the word might mean on index cards. Place one sentence strip in view of all students. (For example: "My brother shrieked when he saw a mouse run across the floor.") Read the sentence aloud. Model for students how to underline the unknown word "shrieked," and then search for clues in the sentence about what the word might mean. Underline the clues in a different color. Then show students the index cards with the possible meanings (one that says "screamed," one that says "whispered," and another that says "laughed"). Have students place the correct index card on top of the unknown word. Then, give students sentence strips of their own and have them do the activity independently, with prompts as needed.

Note: If your student is not able to meet any of the prerequisite skills for this standard, you should assess using the VB-MAPP and start with developmentally appropriate goals.

"What might this word mean?" "Can you think of another word that means the same thing?" "Tell me a clue in the sentence that might help us define this word."

TARGET	INTRODUCED	MASTERED	GENERALIZATION PROBE	
With prompting and support, finds clues in a picture to determine the meaning of a word				
Independently finds clues in a picture to determine the meaning of a word				
Independently finds clues in a picture to determine the meaning of a word when the lesson is not explicitly labeled as "using context clues"				
With prompting and support, finds clues through helping words (such as "like," "called," or "or") to determine the meaning of a word				
Independently finds clues through helping words to determine the meaning of a word				
Independently finds clues through helping words to determine the meaning of a word when the lesson is not explicitly labeled as "using context clues"				

(continued)

Language
Vocabulary Acquisition and Use
L.1.4: L.1.4.a, L.1.4.b, L.1.4.c
L.1.5: L.1.5.a, L.1.5.b, L.1.5.c, L.1.5.d
L.1.6

STUDENT: _____

(L.1.4.a page 2)

With prompting and support, finds clues through known words in the sentence to determine the meaning of a word				
Independently finds clues through known words in the sentence to determine the meaning of a word				
Independently finds clues through known words in the sentence to determine the meaning of a word when the lesson is not explicitly labeled as "using context clues"				
Add additional targets				

⚠ **If your student has not met the prerequisite skills for this standard, drill down to L.K.4.a.**

Procedure and Data Collection: Run 10–20 trials per session with a **Y** or **N** per trial. Graph the overall percentage of the number correct on the Per Opportunity Graph.

Mastery Criterion: 80% correct across three consecutive sessions with two different instructors.

Language
Vocabulary Acquisition and Use
L.1.4: L.1.4.a, L.1.4.b, L.1.4.c
L.1.5: L.1.5.a, L.1.5.b, L.1.5.c, L.1.5.d
L.1.6

STUDENT: _____

L.1.4*

Determine or clarify the meaning of unknown and multiple-meaning words and phrases based on *grade 1 reading and content,* choosing flexibly from an array of strategies.

*This standard is divided into three more specified standards: L.1.4.a, L.1.4.b, and L.1.4.c. Once these three standards have been met, L.1.4 is considered mastered.

L.1.4.b

Use frequently occurring affixes as a clue to the meaning of a word.

Materials: *SpinZone Magnetic Whiteboard Spinners,* Index cards, Sentence strips (not included in kit)

Teaching Procedure: Prior to the lesson, select the prefixes or suffixes you will be introducing. Attach a spinner to the whiteboard. Draw a circle around it and then divide it into three parts and write an affix in each section. Write a target word on the board or on a sentence strip placed in view of all students. Students take turns spinning the spinner, adding the affix to the target word, and then describing the new meaning. For example, if the target word is "teach" and the spinner lands on the suffix "er," the student would say, "teacher" and then, "a teacher is a person who teaches."

"What does the word mean now?" "Can you add a suffix that makes the word mean ___?" "What does this prefix mean?" "Does a prefix come before or after the word?"

TARGET	INTRODUCED	MASTERED	GENERALIZATION PROBE	
Defines one affix				
Adds one affix to one word and explains the meaning of the new word				
Adds one affix to three or more words and explains the meanings of the new words				
Defines three affixes				
Adds at least three affixes to words and explains the meanings of the new words				
Defines five or more affixes				
Adds at least five affixes to words and explains the meanings of the new words				
Encounters a known affix in a novel word and describes what that word might mean				
Add additional target				

If your student has not met the prerequisite skills for this standard, drill down to L.K.4.b.

Procedure and Data Collection: Run 10–20 trials per session with a **Y** or **N** per trial. Graph the overall percentage of the number correct on the Per Opportunity Graph.

Mastery Criterion: 80% correct across three consecutive sessions with two different instructors.

Language
Vocabulary Acquisition and Use
L.1.4: L.1.4.a, L.1.4.b, L.1.4.c
L.1.5: L.1.5.a, L.1.5.b, L.1.5.c, L.1.5.d
L.1.6

STUDENT: _____

L.1.4* Determine or clarify the meaning of unknown and multiple-meaning words and phrases based on *grade 1 reading and content,* choosing flexibly from an array of strategies.

*This standard is divided into three more specified standards: L.1.4.a, L.1.4.b, and L.1.4.c. Once these three standards have been met, L.1.4 is considered mastered.

L.1.4.c Identify frequently occurring root words (e.g., *look*) and their inflectional forms (e.g., *looks, looked, looking*).

Materials: *Sentence Building Dominoes, SpinZone Magnetic Whiteboard Spinners, Talking in Sentences* (page 80)

Teaching Procedure: Prior to the lesson, pull out frequently occurring root words from the *Sentence Building Dominoes.* Also pull out the dominoes that show "s," "es," "ed," and "ing." Label the root word as a "root word" for students. Then add one of the suffix dominoes and ask students what the word means now. Let students create words on their own using the dominoes, and have them describe the meanings of the words as they create them.

"What does the word mean now?" "What can you add to the root word to show it happened yesterday?"

TARGET	INTRODUCED	MASTERED	GENERALIZATION PROBE	
When presented with a word in inflectional form, identifies the root word in 80% of opportunities				
When presented with a root word, adds -s or -es and describes the new meaning				
When presented with a root word, adds -ed and describes the new meaning				
When presented with a root word, adds -ing and describes the new meaning				
Add additional targets				

If your student has not met the prerequisite skills for this standard, drill down to L.K.4.b.

Procedure and Data Collection: Run 10–20 trials per session with a **Y** or **N** per trial. Graph the overall percentage of the number correct on the Per Opportunity Graph.

Mastery Criterion: 80% correct across three consecutive sessions with two different instructors.

Language
Vocabulary Acquisition and Use
L.1.4: L.1.4.a, L.1.4.b, L.1.4.c
L.1.5: L.1.5.a, L.1.5.b, L.1.5.c, L.1.5.d
L.1.6

STUDENT: _____

L.1.5* With guidance and support from adults, demonstrate understanding of word relationships and nuances in word meanings.

*This standard is divided into four more specified standards: L.1.5.a, L.1.5.b, L.1.5.c, and L.1.5.d. Once these four standards have been met, L.1.5 is considered mastered.

L.1.5.a Sort words into categories (e.g., colors, clothing) to gain a sense of the concepts the categories represent.

Materials: *SpinZone Magnetic Whiteboard Spinners, Sentence Building Dominoes,* Index cards (not included in kit)

Teaching Procedure: Prior to the lesson, prepare the names of categories you want your students to focus on for that day such as food, clothing, vehicles, and school supplies. Write the names of several items for each category on individual index cards. Attach a spinner to the whiteboard. Draw a circle around it, divide it into the appropriate number of parts, and then write a category in each section. Students take turns spinning the spinner and then selecting an index card that names an item that fits in that category. To make the activity more challenging, select items that can fit in more than one category (e.g., create categories of "blue," "yellow," "round," and "big"). After students have placed an item in a category, challenge them to show another category it could fit into.

"Can you find an item that is a type of clothing?" "In what category does the pencil belong?" "Think of another item that might fit in that category."

TARGET	INTRODUCED	MASTERED	GENERALIZATION PROBE	
When presented with a group of five to six words, sorts those words into two given categories				
When presented with a group of nine to 12 words, sorts those words into three given categories				
When presented with a group of nine to 12 words, sorts those words into four given categories				
When presented with a group of 12 to 15 words, sorts those words into four or more given categories				
When presented with a group of five to six words, generates two categories and sorts the words correctly				
When presented with a group of nine to 12 words, generates three categories and sorts the words correctly				
When presented with a group of nine to 12 words, generates four categories and sorts the words correctly				

(continued)

Language
Vocabulary Acquisition and Use
L.1.4: L.1.4.a, L.1.4.b, L.1.4.c
L.1.5: L.1.5.a, L.1.5.b, L.1.5.c, L.1.5.d
L.1.6

STUDENT: _____

(L.1.5.a page 2)

When presented with a group of 12 to 15 words, generates four or more categories and sorts the words correctly				
Add additional targets				

 If your student has not met the prerequisite skills for this standard, drill down to L.K.5.a.

 Procedure and Data Collection: Run 10–20 trials per session with a **Y** or **N** per trial.
Graph the overall percentage of the number correct on the Per Opportunity Graph.

Mastery Criterion: 80% correct across three consecutive sessions with two different instructors.

Language
Vocabulary Acquisition and Use
L.1.4: L.1.4.a, L.1.4.b, L.1.4.c
L.1.5: L.1.5.a, L.1.5.b, L.1.5.c, L.1.5.d
L.1.6

STUDENT: _____

L.1.5* With guidance and support from adults, demonstrate understanding of word relationships and nuances in word meanings.

*This standard is divided into four more specified standards: L.1.5.a, L.1.5.b, L.1.5.c, and L.1.5.d. Once these four standards have been met, L.1.5 is considered mastered.

L.1.5.b Define words by category and by one or more key attributes (e.g., a *duck* is a bird that swims; a *tiger* is a large cat with stripes).

Materials: *Sentence Building Dominoes, Talking in Sentences, Big Box of Word Chunks, SpinZone Magnetic Whiteboard Spinners,* Pictures from classroom books or other materials (not included in kit)

Teaching Procedure: Prior to the lesson, gather several pictures of familiar items. Write on the dry-erase board, "Two steps for defining words: (1) name the category (2) give an attribute." Read the steps aloud to students and then hold up one of the pictures and model the procedure for them. For example, hold up a picture of a car and say, "A car is a vehicle (pointing to step one when you say "vehicle") that has four wheels" (point to step two when you say "has four wheels"). Show another picture and have students complete the activity. Following your model, the student should point to each step as he/she defines the word. Then distribute pictures to all the students and let them practice.

"Tell me more." "Can you define the word ___?" "Think of another attribute."

TARGET	INTRODUCED	MASTERED	GENERALIZATION PROBE	
Defines a word by its category when presented with a picture for three or more pictures				
Defines a word by its category when presented with a picture for five or more pictures				
Defines a word by its category and at least one attribute when presented with a picture for five or more pictures				
Defines a word by its category when presented with a picture for 10 or more pictures, and identifies at least two categories across all pictures				
Defines a word by its category and at least one attribute when presented with a picture for 10 or more pictures, and identifies at least two categories across all pictures				
Defines a word by its category when presented with a picture for 25 or more pictures, and identifies at least three categories across all pictures				

(continued)

Language
Vocabulary Acquisition and Use
L.1.4: L.1.4.a, L.1.4.b, L.1.4.c
L.1.5: L.1.5.a, L.1.5.b, L.1.5.c, L.1.5.d
L.1.6

STUDENT: _____

(L.1.5.b page 2)

Defines a word by its category and at least one attribute when presented with a picture for 25 or more pictures, and identifies at least three categories across all pictures			
Defines a word by its category when presented with a picture for 50 or more pictures, and identifies at least five categories across all pictures			
Defines a word by its category and at least one attribute when presented with a picture for 50 or more pictures, and identifies at least three categories across all pictures			
Defines a word by its category and at least one attribute when presented with a picture for 50 or more pictures, using at least five categories			
When prompted, provides a second attribute as part of a definition for at least five pictures			
Independently provides a second attribute as part of a definition for at least five pictures			
Defines a word by its category when presented with a written/oral word for three or more words			
Defines a word by its category when presented with a written/oral word for five or more words			
Defines a word by its category and at least one attribute when presented with a written/oral word for five or more words			
Defines a word by its category when presented with a written/oral word for 10 or more words, and identifies at least two categories across all words			
Defines a word by its category and at least one attribute when presented with a written/oral word for 10 or more words, and identifies at least two categories across all words			
Defines a word by its category and at least one attribute when presented with a written/oral word for 10 or more words, using at least two categories			
Defines a word by its category when presented with a written/oral word for 25 or more words, and identifies at least three categories across all words			
Defines a word by its category and at least one attribute when presented with a written/oral word for 25 or more words, and identifies at least three categories across all words			

(continued)

Language
Vocabulary Acquisition and Use
L.1.4: L.1.4.a, L.1.4.b, L.1.4.c
L.1.5: L.1.5.a, L.1.5.b, L.1.5.c, L.1.5.d
L.1.6

STUDENT: _____

(L.1.5.b page 3)

Defines a word by its category when presented with a written/oral word for 50 or more words, and identifies at least three categories across all words				
Defines a word by its category and at least one attribute when presented with a written/oral word for 50 or more pictures, and identifies at least three categories across all words				
Defines a word by its category and at least one attribute when presented with a written/oral word for 50 or more pictures, and identifies at least five categories across all words				
When prompted, provides a second attribute as part of a definition for at least five words				
Independently provides a second attribute as part of a definition for at least five words				
Add additional targets				

 If your student has not met the prerequisite skills for this standard, drill down to L.K.5.a.

 Procedure and Data Collection: Run 10–20 trials per session with a **Y** or **N** per trial. Graph the overall percentage of the number correct on the Per Opportunity Graph.

Mastery Criterion: 80% correct across three consecutive sessions with two different instructors.

Language
Vocabulary Acquisition and Use
L.1.4: L.1.4.a, L.1.4.b, L.1.4.c
L.1.5: L.1.5.a, L.1.5.b, L.1.5.c, L.1.5.d
L.1.6

STUDENT: _____

L.1.5*

With guidance and support from adults, demonstrate understanding of word relationships and nuances in word meanings.

This standard is divided into four more specified standards: L.1.5.a, L.1.5.b, L.1.5.c, and L.1.5.d. Once these four standards have been met, L.1.5 is considered mastered.

L.1.5.c

Identify real-life connections between words and their use (e.g., note places at home that are *cozy*).

Materials: *Big Box of Word Chunks*

Teaching Procedure: Place several pieces from the *Big Box of Word Chunks* on the table within reach of all students. Model how to put together two pieces to create a word (such as connect "f" and "un" to create the word "fun"). Then, use the word to describe a real-life connection to the school day (e.g., "Playing *Red Light Green Light* at recess was really fun"). Let students volunteer to create their own words and use them in a sentence to connect the word to a real-life item or experience.

"Can you use that word in a sentence?" "Describe something in the school using that word." "Tell me about something lucky that has happened to you."

TARGET	INTRODUCED	MASTERED	GENERALIZATION PROBE	
Identifies one exemplar of five or more real-life connections to words				
Identifies one exemplar of 10 or more real-life connections to words				
Identifies two exemplars of five or more real-life connections to words				
Identifies two exemplars of 10 or more real-life connections to words				
Identifies two exemplars of 25 or more real-life connections to words				
Identifies three exemplars of 10 or more real-life connections to words				
Identifies three exemplars of 25 or more real-life connections to words				
Add additional target				

If your student has not met the prerequisite skills for this standard, drill down to L.K.5.c.

Procedure and Data Collection: Run 10–20 trials per session with a **Y** or **N** per trial. Graph the overall percentage of the number correct on the Per Opportunity Graph.

Mastery Criterion: 80% correct across three consecutive sessions with two different instructors.

Language
Vocabulary Acquisition and Use
L.1.4: L.1.4.a, L.1.4.b, L.1.4.c
L.1.5: L.1.5.a, L.1.5.b, L.1.5.c, L.1.5.d
L.1.6

L.1.5* With guidance and support from adults, demonstrate understanding of word relationships and nuances in word meanings.

*This standard is divided into four more specified standards: L.1.5.a, L.1.5.b, L.1.5.c, and L.1.5.d. Once these four standards have been met, L.1.5 is considered mastered.

L.1.5.d Distinguish shades of meaning among verbs differing in manner (e.g., *look, peek, glance, stare, glare, scowl*) and adjectives differing in intensity (e.g., *large, gigantic*) by defining or choosing them or by acting out the meanings.

 Materials: *SpinZone Magnetic Whiteboard Spinners, Write-on/Wipe-off Crayons,* Index cards (not included in kit)

 Teaching Procedure: Prior to the lesson, prepare the names of several similar verbs and similar adjectives. Attach a spinner to the whiteboard. Draw a circle around it, and then divide it into the appropriate number of parts for your lesson. In each section, write a set of similar verbs or similar adjectives. For example, one part might say "look, peek." Spin the spinner and model for students how to act out the two words to demonstrate their differences in meaning. Students take turns spinning the spinner and acting out and/or verbally defining the words in each set. You can also utilize index cards. For each index card, write one verb or adjective on one side, then a similar verb or adjective on the other side. The student looks at the word, acts it out, then flips the card and acts out the similar word.

 "Can you show me with your hands what large looks like?" "Show me looking. Now show me peeking."

TARGET	INTRODUCED	MASTERED	GENERALIZATION PROBE	
Acts out the differences between one set of two verbs that have similar meanings				
Acts out the differences between three sets of two verbs that have similar meanings				
Acts out the differences between five sets of two verbs that have similar meanings				
Acts out the differences between a novel set of two verbs that have similar meanings				
Acts out the differences between one set of two adjectives that have similar meanings but differ in intensity				
Acts out the differences between three sets of two adjectives that have similar meanings but differ in intensity				

(continued)

Language
Vocabulary Acquisition and Use
L.1.4: L.1.4.a, L.1.4.b, L.1.4.c
L.1.5: L.1.5.a, L.1.5.b, L.1.5.c, L.1.5.d
L.1.6

STUDENT: _____

(L.1.5.d page 2)

Acts out the differences between five sets of two adjectives that have similar meanings but differ in intensity				
Acts out the differences between a novel set of two adjectives that have similar meanings but differ in intensity				
Add additional targets				

If your student has not met the prerequisite skills for this standard, drill down to L.K.5.d.

Procedure and Data Collection: Run 10–20 trials per session with a **Y** or **N** per trial.
Graph the overall percentage of the number correct on the Per Opportunity Graph.

Mastery Criterion: 80% correct across three consecutive sessions with two different instructors.

Language
Vocabulary Acquisition and Use
L.1.4: L.1.4.a, L.1.4.b, L.1.4.c
L.1.5: L.1.5.a, L.1.5.b, L.1.5.c, L.1.5.d
L.1.6

L.1.6

Use words and phrases acquired through conversations, reading and being read to, and responding to texts, including using frequently occurring conjunctions to signal simple relationships (e.g., *because*).

Materials: Classroom reading materials, Visual, textual, or gestural prompts during conversation (not included in kit)

Teaching Procedure: Prior to a reading activity, select the word(s) you want each student to focus on acquiring during that lesson. Prepare questions in advance for the student to answer using the target word. For example, if your target word is "because," the questions you prepare might look like this: "What did the girl do?" (She got in the boat.) "Why did she get in the boat?" (Because she had to get across the river.) "Can you put the two sentences together?" (She got in the boat because she had to get across the river.) During the lesson, ask the questions you have prepared to help each student use the target words and phrases appropriately.

Note: If your student is not able to meet any of the prerequisite skills for this standard, you should assess using the VB-MAPP and start with developmentally appropriate goals.

"Can you use the word from the text?" "Describe it better." "How did the author describe it?"

TARGET	INTRODUCED	MASTERED	GENERALIZATION PROBE	
During a story activity, responds to questions using one word/phrase from the activity				
During a story activity, responds to questions using three or more words/phrases from the activity				
During a conversation uses one or more words/ phrases introduced in that conversation				
During a story activity, responds to at least one question using a conjunction				
During a story activity, responds to at least three questions using a conjunction				
During a conversation, responds to at least one question or statement using a conjunction				
During a conversation, responds to at least three questions or statements using a conjunction				
During a conversation, responds to at least three questions or statements using a conjunction, using at least two different conjunctions				

(continued)

Language
Vocabulary Acquisition and Use
L.1.4: L.1.4.a, L.1.4.b, L.1.4.c
L.1.5: L.1.5.a, L.1.5.b, L.1.5.c, L.1.5.d
L.1.6

STUDENT: _____

(L.1.6 page 2)

Add additional targets				

If your student has not met the prerequisite skills for this standard, drill down to L.K.6.

Procedure and Data Collection: Run 10–20 trials per session with a **Y** or **N** per trial. Graph the overall percentage of the number correct on the Per Opportunity Graph.

Mastery Criterion: 80% correct across three consecutive sessions with two different instructors.

OPERATIONS AND ALGEBRAIC THINKING OVERVIEW

· Represent and solve problems involving addition and subtraction

· Understand and apply properties of operations and the relationship between addition and subtraction

· Add and subtract within 20

· Work with addition and subtraction equations

CCSS CODE	STANDARD
1.OA.A.1	Use addition and subtraction within 20 to solve word problems involving situations of adding to, taking from, putting together, taking apart, and comparing, with unknowns in all positions, e.g., by using objects, drawings, and equations with a symbol for the unknown number to represent the problem.[1]
1.OA.A.2	Solve word problems that call for addition of three whole numbers whose sum is less than or equal to 20, e.g., by using objects, drawings, and equations with a symbol for the unknown number to represent the problem.
1.OA.B.3	Apply properties of operations as strategies to add and subtract.[2] Examples: If $8 + 3 = 11$ is known, then $3 + 8 = 11$ is also known. (Commutative property of addition.) To add $2 + 6 + 4$, the second two numbers can be added to make a ten, so $2 + 6 + 4 = 2 + 10 = 12$. (Associative property of addition.)
1.OA.B.4	Understand subtraction as an unknown-addend problem. For example, subtract $10 - 8$ by finding the number that makes 10 when added to 8.
1.OA.C.5	Relate counting to addition and subtraction (e.g., by counting on 2 to add 2).
1.OA.C.6	Add and subtract within 20, demonstrating fluency for addition and subtraction within 10. Use strategies such as counting on; making ten (e.g., $8 + 6 = 8 + 2 + 4 = 10 + 4 = 14$); decomposing a number leading to a ten (e.g., $13 - 4 = 13 - 3 - 1 = 10 - 1 = 9$); using the relationship between addition and subtraction (e.g., knowing that $8 + 4 = 12$, one knows $12 - 8 = 4$); and creating equivalent but easier or known sums (e.g., adding $6 + 7$ by creating the known equivalent $6 + 6 + 1 = 12 + 1 = 13$).
1.OA.D.7	Understand the meaning of the equal sign, and determine if equations involving addition and subtraction are true or false. For example, which of the following equations are true and which are false? $6 = 6$, $7 = 8 - 1$, $5 + 2 = 2 + 5$, $4 + 1 = 5 + 2$.
1.OA.D.8	Determine the unknown whole number in an addition or subtraction equation relating three whole numbers. For example, determine the unknown number that makes the equation true in each of the equations $8 + ? = 11$, $5 = \_ - 3$, $6 + 6$

[1] *See Mathematics Glossary Table 1, Page 22*

[2] *Students need not use formal terms for these properties.*

(continued)

KIT MATERIALS

- *Make a Splash 120 Mat Floor Game*: 1.OA.A.1, 1.OA.B.4, 1.OA.D.8
- *Ten-Frame Trains*: 1.OA.A.1, 1.OA.A.2, 1.OA.B.3, 1.OA.B.4, 1.OA.C.5, 1.OA.C.6
- *Working with Ten-Frames*: 1.OA.A.1, 1.OA.A.2, 1.OA.B.3, 1.OA.B.4, 1.OA.C.5, 1.OA.C.6
- *Unifix Cubes*: 1.OA.A.1, 1.OA.A.2, 1.OA.B.4, 1.OA.C.5, 1.OA.C.6, 1.OA.D.7, 1.OA.D.8
- *Mathematics with Unifix Cubes*: 1.OA.A.1, 1.OA.A.2, 1.OA.B.4, 1.OA.C.5, 1.OA.C.6, 1.OA.D.7, 1.OA.D.8
- *Thinking Mats*: 1.OA.A.2, 1.OA.B.3, 1.OA.D.7, 1.OA.D.8
- *120 Number Mats*: 1.OA.C.5
- *Write-on/Wipe-off Crayons*: 1.OA.B.3, 1.OA.C.5, 1.OA.D.7

CLASSROOM MATERIALS AND ACTIVITIES

- Number lines
- Math-related storybooks
- Blocks for counting and comparing values
- Common objects in the classroom
- Community walk to find groups of ten

TIP FOR GENERALIZATION

Play the game "Fifteen" with your students. Students should play in pairs. Make a 3-by-3 grid for each pair. Put the numbers 1–9 in the boxes in any order you wish. Give each student game pieces which can be pieces of construction paper, pawns, counters, etc. Students take turns covering a number on the grid. The first player to cover up numbers that add up to 15 wins. If a player goes over 15, they "go bust." If no one can get 15, it's called a "scratch" and a new round is started.

Operations and Algebraic Thinking
Represent and solve problems involving
addition and subtraction
1.OA.A.1, 1.OA.A.2

STUDENT: _____

1.OA.A.1 Use addition and subtraction within 20 to solve word problems involving situations of adding to, taking from, putting together, taking apart, and comparing, with unknowns in all positions, e.g., by using objects, drawings, and equations with a symbol for the unknown number to represent the problem.[1]

[1] *See Mathematics Glossary Table 1, Page 22*

Materials: *Unifix Cubes, Working with Ten-Frames,* Mathematics with Unifix Cubes, Ten-Frame Trains, Make a Splash 120 Mat Floor Game

Teaching Procedure: Prior to the lesson, create several word problems that require addition and subtraction within 20. Give each student several *Unifix Cubes* in two colors. Have them read or listen to the word problem, then show the answer using their cubes. For example, a student has blue and red cubes and the word problem states "Steven has 7 cars. Alan gives him 5 more. How many does Steven have altogether?" The student can attach 7 blue cubes to 5 red cubes to show a total of 12. The "Sum to 20" activity on pages 66–67 of *Working with Ten-Frames* is also an excellent activity for practicing skills for this standard.

"Are we using subtraction or addition to solve this problem?" "Draw a picture to show how to solve the problem." "Show me how you found the answer."

TARGET	INTRODUCED	MASTERED	GENERALIZATION PROBE	
Uses objects to solve word problems requiring addition within 20 correctly in 80% of opportunities				
Uses drawings to solve word problems requiring addition within 20 correctly in 80% of opportunities				
Uses equations to solve word problems requiring addition within 20 correctly in 80% of opportunities				
Uses a variety of methods to solve word problems requiring addition within 20 correctly in 80% of opportunities				
Uses a variety of methods to solve word problems requiring addition within 20 with unknown numbers in all positions correctly in 80% of opportunities				
Uses objects to solve word problems requiring subtraction within 20 correctly in 80% of opportunities				
Uses drawings to solve word problems requiring subtraction within 20 correctly in 80% of opportunities				
Uses equations to solve word problems requiring subtraction within 20 correctly in 80% of opportunities				

(continued)

Operations and Algebraic Thinking
Represent and solve problems involving
addition and subtraction
1.OA.A.1, 1.OA.A.2

STUDENT: _____

(1.OA.A.1 page 2)

Uses a variety of methods to solve word problems requiring subtraction within 20 correctly in 80% of opportunities				
Uses a variety of methods to solve word problems requiring subtraction within 20 with unknown numbers in all positions correctly in 80% of opportunities				
Uses a variety of methods to solve word problems requiring a random mix of addition and subtraction within 20 correctly in 80% of opportunities				
Add additional targets				

 If your student has not met the prerequisite skills for this standard, drill down to K.OA.A.1.

 Procedure and Data Collection: Run 10–20 trials per session with a **Y** or **N** per trial. Graph the overall percentage of the number correct on the Per Opportunity Graph.

Mastery Criterion: 80% correct across three consecutive sessions with two different instructors.

Operations and Algebraic Thinking
Represent and solve problems involving
addition and subtraction
1.OA.A.1, 1.OA.A.2

STUDENT: _____

1.OA.A.2 Solve word problems that call for addition of three whole numbers whose sum is less than or equal to 20, e.g., by using objects, drawings, and equations with a symbol for the unknown number to represent the problem.

Materials: *Working with Ten-Frames, Ten-Frame Trains,* Unifix Cubes, Mathematics with Unifix Cubes, Thinking Mats

Teaching Procedure: Prior to the lesson, refer to page 149 of the *Working with Ten-Frames* workbook. If necessary, reproduce page 149 for students to refer to when solving word problems. Provide each student with two *Ten-Frame Trains.* For larger classes, you may need to have students work in pairs. Model for students how to use the ten-frame to help solve the word problem. After modeling, guide students through a second problem, requiring them to imitate each step of solving the problem using the ten-frames. Then allow students to practice solving additional problems on their own.

"Show me how to solve this problem." "Can you make a drawing to find the answer?"

TARGET	INTRODUCED	MASTERED	GENERALIZATION PROBE	
Uses objects to solve word problems requiring addition within 20 of three single-digit numbers correctly in 80% of opportunities				
Uses drawings to solve word problems requiring addition within 20 of three single-digit numbers correctly in 80% of opportunities				
Uses equations to solve word problems requiring addition within 20 of three single-digit numbers correctly in 80% of opportunities				
Uses objects to solve word problems requiring addition within 20 of two single-digit numbers and one double-digit number correctly in 80% of opportunities				
Uses drawings to solve word problems requiring addition within 20 of two single-digit numbers and one double-digit number correctly in 80% of opportunities				
Uses equations to solve word problems requiring addition within 20 of two single-digit numbers and one double-digit number correctly in 80% of opportunities				

(continued)

Operations and Algebraic Thinking
Represent and solve problems involving
addition and subtraction
1.OA.A.1, 1.OA.A.2

STUDENT: _____

(1.OA.A.2 page 2)

Add additional targets				

If your student has not met the prerequisite skills for this standard, drill down to K.OA.A.2.

Procedure and Data Collection: Run 10-20 trials per session with a **Y** or **N** per trial.
Graph the overall percentage of the number correct on the Per Opportunity Graph.

Mastery Criterion: 80% correct across three consecutive sessions with two different instructors.

Operations and Algebraic Thinking
Understand and apply properties of
operations and the relationship between
addition and subtraction
1.OA.B.3, 1.OA.B.4

STUDENT: _____

1.OA.B.3

Apply properties of operations as strategies to add and subtract.*

Examples: If 8 + 3 = 11 is known, then 3 + 8 = 11 is also known. (Commutative property of addition.) To add 2 + 6 + 4, the second two numbers can be added to make a ten, so 2 + 6 + 4 = 2 + 10 = 12. (Associative property of addition.)

*Note: Students need not use formal terms for these properties.

Materials: *Thinking Mats, Write-on/Wipe-off Crayons, Ten-Frame Trains, Working with Ten-Frames*

Teaching Procedure: Prepare the "Super Scoops" mat from the *Thinking Mats* and have wipe-away crayons available for each student. When teaching the commutative property of addition, demonstrate for students how to make two ice cream cones using the materials. For example, you might place four scoops of ice cream on one cone and two scoops of ice cream on the second cone. Have students help you count the total number of scoops. Next, switch the order of the two cones (with two scoops on the first cone and four scoops on the second) and ask students if it is the same number of total scoops. Write the two equations for all students to see (4 + 2 = 6 and 2 + 4 = 6). Allow students time to explore the materials and create and write their own pairs of equations demonstrating the commutative property of addition. The "Super Scoops" mat can also be used to teach and practice the associative property of addition.

"We know 2 + 4 = 6. What is 4 + 2?" "Add them up." "Let's add one number at a time."

TARGET	INTRODUCED	MASTERED	GENERALIZATION PROBE	
With prompting and support, demonstrates commutative property of addition using manipulatives				
Independently demonstrates commutative property of addition using manipulatives				
With prompting and support, demonstrates commutative property of addition through drawing or writing equations				
Independently demonstrates commutative property of addition through drawing or writing equations				
With prompting and support, verbally demonstrates commutative property of addition without the use of manipulatives, drawing, or writing equations (i.e., responds to: If 2 + 4 = 6, then what is 4 + 2?)				
Independently verbally demonstrates commutative property of addition without the use of manipulatives, drawing, or writing equations (i.e., responds to: If 2 + 4 = 6, then what is 4 + 2?)				

(continued)

Operations and Algebraic Thinking
Understand and apply properties of
operations and the relationship between
addition and subtraction
1.OA.B.3, 1.OA.B.4

STUDENT: _____

(1.OA.B.3 page 2)

With prompting and support, demonstrates associative property of addition using manipulatives				
Independently demonstrates associative property of addition using manipulatives				
With prompting and support, demonstrates associative property of addition through drawing or writing equations				
Independently demonstrates associative property of addition through drawing or writing equations				
With prompting and support, verbally demonstrates associative property of addition without the use of manipulatives, drawing, or writing equations (i.e., responds to: What is 2 + 6 + 4?)				
Independently verbally demonstrates associative property of addition without the use of manipulatives, drawing, or writing equations (i.e., responds to: What is 2 + 6 + 4?)				
Add additional targets				

 If your student has not met the prerequisite skills for this standard, drill down to **K.OA.A.1, K.OA.A.3.**

 Procedure and Data Collection: Run 10–20 trials per session with a **Y** or **N** per trial.
Graph the overall percentage of the number correct on the Per Opportunity Graph.

Mastery Criterion: 80% correct across three consecutive sessions with two different instructors.

Operations and Algebraic Thinking
Understand and apply properties of
operations and the relationship between
addition and subtraction
1.OA.B.3, 1.OA.B.4

1.OA.B.4 Understand subtraction as an unknown-addend problem. For example, subtract 10 – 8 by finding the number that makes 10 when added to 8.

Materials: *Mathematics with Unifix Cubes, Unifix Cubes, Ten-Frame Trains, Working with Ten-Frames, Make a Splash 120 Mat Floor Game*

Teaching Procedure: Make copies of the "Unifix 1–10 Stair" and "Missing Addend Cards" from pages 32–34 in the *Mathematics with Unifix Cubes* book. Split students into pairs and provide each student with 55 *Unifix Cubes* of one color. Have students complete Activity 1 from page 31 in the *Mathematics with Unifix Cubes* workbook. Have students share the equations they create, and write subtraction problems that are part of each fact family.

"Can we use addition to solve that subtraction problem?" "We know 2 + 8 = 10, so 10 – 8 must equal ___?"

TARGET	INTRODUCED	MASTERED	GENERALIZATION PROBE
With prompting and support, solves a subtraction problem by using an unknown addend problem for subtraction problems within five			
Independently solves a subtraction problem by using an unknown addend problem for subtraction problems within five			
Independently solves a subtraction problem by using an unknown addend problem for subtraction problems within 10			
With prompting and support, solves a subtraction problem by using an unknown addend problem through drawing or writing equations			
Independently solves a subtraction problem by using an unknown addend problem through drawing or writing equations			
With prompting and support, verbally solves a subtraction problem by using an unknown addend problem without the use of manipulatives, drawing, or writing equations (i.e., responds to: If 2 + 8 = 10, then 10 – 8 = ___?)			
Independently verbally solves a subtraction problem by using an unknown addend problem without the use of manipulatives, drawing, or writing equations (i.e., responds to: If 2 + 8 = 10, then 10 – 8 = ___?)			

(continued)

Operations and Algebraic Thinking
Understand and apply properties of
operations and the relationship between
addition and subtraction
1.OA.B.3, 1.OA.B.4

STUDENT: _____

(1.OA.B.4 page 2)

Add additional targets				

 If your student has not met the prerequisite skills for this standard, drill down to K.OA.A.3.

 Procedure and Data Collection: Run 10–20 trials per session with a **Y** or **N** per trial.
Graph the overall percentage of the number correct on the Per Opportunity Graph.

Mastery Criterion: 80% correct across three consecutive sessions with two different instructors.

STUDENT: _____

1.OA.C.5   Relate counting to addition and subtraction (e.g., by counting on 2 to add 2).

Materials: *120 Number Mats, Write-on/Wipe-off Crayons,* Ten-Frame Trains, Working with Ten-Frames, Unifix Cubes

Teaching Procedure: Provide each student with a *120 Number Mat* and *Write-On/Wipe-off Crayons.* Present an addition problem, such as 42 + 3. Tell students they can "count on" to discover the answer. Demonstrate for students how to circle the first addend, and then put a mark on each space they count. For example, circle the 42 on the number mat, then mark 43, 44, and 45 as count "1, 2, 3." When you get to the '3,' circle the number you land on. Tell students, "42 plus 3 equals 45." Present another addition problem and allow students to try "counting on" independently. Once students have mastered counting on with addition, introduce using the same concept with subtraction.

"Can you count on?" "How can we solve this problem?" "Let's count."

TARGET	INTRODUCED	MASTERED	GENERALIZATION PROBE
With prompting and support, uses counting to solve addition problems with the use of manipulatives or a number mat			
Independently uses counting to solve addition problems with the use of manipulatives or a number mat			
With prompting and support, uses counting to solve addition problems with the use of drawing or writing			
Independently uses counting to solve addition problems with the use of drawing or writing			
With prompting and support, uses counting to solve subtraction problems with the use of manipulatives or a number mat			
Independently uses counting to solve subtraction problems with the use of manipulatives or a number mat			
With prompting and support, uses counting to solve subtraction problems with the use of drawing or writing			
Independently uses counting to solve subtraction problems with the use of drawing or writing			
Independently uses counting to solve a mix of addition and subtraction problems			

(continued)

Add additional targets				

If your student has not met the prerequisite skills for this standard, drill down to K.OA.A.1, K.OA.A.3.

Procedure and Data Collection: Run 10–20 trials per session with a **Y** or **N** per trial.
Graph the overall percentage of the number correct on the Per Opportunity Graph.

Mastery Criterion: 80% correct across three consecutive sessions with two different instructors.

STUDENT: _____

1.OA.C.6 Add and subtract within 20, demonstrating fluency for addition and subtraction within 10. Use strategies such as counting on; making ten (e.g., 8 + 6 = 8 + 2 + 4 = 10 + 4 = 14); decomposing a number leading to a ten (e.g., 13 − 4 = 13 − 3 − 1 = 10 − 1 = 9); using the relationship between addition and subtraction (e.g., knowing that 8 + 4 = 12, one knows 12 − 8 = 4); and creating equivalent but easier or known sums (e.g., adding 6 + 7 by creating the known equivalent 6 + 6 + 1 = 12 + 1 = 13).

Materials: *Working with Ten-Frames, Ten-Frame Trains, Unifix Cubes, Mathematics with Unifix Cubes*

Teaching Procedure: Prepare the "Where Are You?" activity on pages 60–61 of *Working with Ten-Frames*. (Be sure to make four copies of the Ten-Frame Cards on page 114.) Put students in pairs and tell them they are going to work together to find pairs that add up to twenty. Demonstrate how to do this with a paraprofessional or a student. Remind students to write down the equations they find.

"How can we solve this problem?" "Can you count on?" "Can we use addition to solve that subtraction problem?"

TARGET	INTRODUCED	MASTERED	GENERALIZATION PROBE	
With prompting and support, utilizes a variety of strategies to solve addition problems within 10				
Independently utilizes a variety of strategies to solve addition problems within 10				
With prompting and support, utilizes a variety of strategies to solve subtraction problems within 10				
Independently utilizes a variety of strategies to solve subtraction problems within 10				
With prompting and support, utilizes a variety of strategies to solve addition problems within 20				
Independently utilizes a variety of strategies to solve addition problems within 20				
With prompting and support, utilizes a variety of strategies to solve subtraction problems within 20				
Independently utilizes a variety of strategies to solve subtraction problems within 20				
With prompting and support, utilizes a variety of strategies to solve a mix of addition and subtraction problems within 20				
Independently utilizes a variety of strategies to solve a mix of addition and subtraction problems within 20				

(continued)

Add additional targets				

 If your student has not met the prerequisite skills for this standard, drill down to K.OA.A.1, K.OA.A.3, K.OA.A.5.

 Procedure and Data Collection: Run 10–20 trials per session with a **Y** or **N** per trial.
Graph the overall percentage of the number correct on the Per Opportunity Graph.

Mastery Criterion: 80% correct across three consecutive sessions with two different instructors.

STUDENT: _____

1.OA.D.7 Understand the meaning of the equal sign, and determine if equations involving addition and subtraction are true or false. For example, which of the following equations are true and which are false? $6 = 6, 7 = 8 - 1, 5 + 2 = 2 + 5, 4 + 1 = 5 + 2$.

 Materials: *Thinking Mats, Write-On/Wipe-off Crayons,* Unifix Cubes, *Mathematics with Unifix Cubes*

 Teaching Procedure: Prepare the "Penguin Paths" mat from the *Thinking Mats* and have wipe-away crayons for each student. Prior to the lesson, you may want to color code the backs of the equation cards so you can easily select the appropriate difficulty level for each student. To begin, tell students that "equals" means "same." Place a large picture of an equal sign on the table in view of all students. Use manipulatives to introduce the basic definition by placing the same number of manipulatives on each side of the equal sign. Provide examples and non-examples to help students understand the concept. After providing several practices with a variety of examples, allow students who are demonstrating mastery to play "Penguin Paths" and provide individualized attention to those students who are struggling with the concept.

 "Are these two numbers equal?" "What does equal mean?" "True or false?"

TARGET	INTRODUCED	MASTERED	GENERALIZATION PROBE	
When asked "What does equal mean?" responds, "the same"				
When presented with two of the same numbers, amounts, or quantities, labels them as "equal"				
When presented with equations involving addition, states whether or not the two equations are equal				
When presented with equations involving subtraction, states whether or not the two equations are equal				
When presented with equations involving addition and/or subtraction, states whether or not the two equations are equal				
When presented with equations involving addition and/or subtraction, can accurately respond "true" or "false" to "these two are equal"				
Add additional target				

 If your student has not met the prerequisite skills for this standard, drill down to K.OA.A.1, K.OA.A.4.

 Procedure and Data Collection: Run 10–20 trials per session with a **Y** or **N** per trial. Graph the overall percentage of the number correct on the Per Opportunity Graph.

Mastery Criterion: 80% correct across three consecutive sessions with two different instructors.

1.OA.D.8 Determine the unknown whole number in an addition or subtraction equation relating three whole numbers. For example, determine the unknown number that makes the equation true in each of the equations $8 + ? = 11$, $5 = \_ - 3$, $6 + 6 = \_$.

Materials: *Make a Splash 120 Mat Floor Game*, *Unifix Cubes*, *Mathematics with Unifix Cubes*, *Thinking Mats*

Teaching Procedure: Place the *Make a Splash 120 Mat Floor Game* in view of all students. Set aside Markers and Square Frames from the floor game. Tell students you are going to do some mystery math. Show an equation, such as $8 + ? = 11$. Place square frames on the 8 and the 11 on the mat. Model for students how to count on to complete the equation. Provide two to three more examples, then provide equations for students to solve on their own using the floor mat. Remind students to record their solutions to each equation.

"How can we find the solution?" "Let's count on." "Subtract."

TARGET	INTRODUCED	MASTERED	GENERALIZATION PROBE	
With prompting and support, determines the unknown whole number in an addition equation for solutions within 10 using manipulatives				
Independently determines the unknown whole number in an addition equation for solutions within 10 using manipulatives				
With prompting and support, determines the unknown whole number in a subtraction equation for solutions within 10 using manipulatives				
Independently determines the unknown whole number in a subtraction equation for solutions within 10 using manipulatives				
With prompting and support, determines the unknown whole number in an addition equation for solutions within 20 using manipulatives				
Independently determines the unknown whole number in an addition equation for solutions within 20 using manipulatives				
With prompting and support, determines the unknown whole number in a subtraction equation for solutions within 20 using manipulatives				
Independently determines the unknown whole number in a subtraction equation for solutions within 20 using manipulatives				

(continued)

STUDENT: _____

(1.OA.D.8 page 2)

With prompting and support, uses a variety of strategies to determine the unknown whole number in an equation with three whole numbers				
Independently uses a variety of strategies to determine the unknown whole number in an equation with three whole numbers				
Add additional targets				

If your student has not met the prerequisite skills for this standard, drill down to K.OA.A.2, K.OA.A.3, K.OA.A.4.

Procedure and Data Collection: Run 10-20 trials per session with a **Y** or **N** per trial.
Graph the overall percentage of the number correct on the Per Opportunity Graph.

Mastery Criterion: 80% correct across three consecutive sessions with two different instructors.

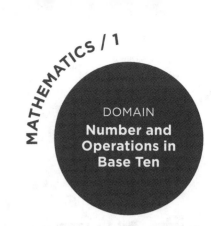

NUMBER AND OPERATIONS IN BASE TEN OVERVIEW

· Extend the counting sequence
· Understand place value
· Use place value understanding and properties of operations to add and subtract

CCSS CODE	STANDARD
1.NBT.A.1	Count to 120, starting at any number less than 120. In this range, read and write numerals and represent a number of objects with a written numeral.
1.NBT.B.2	Understand that the two digits of a two-digit number represent amounts of tens and ones. Understand the following as special cases:
1.NBT.B.2.a	10 can be thought of as a bundle of ten ones—called a "ten."
1.NBT.B.2.b	The numbers from 11 to 19 are composed of a ten and one, two, three, four, five, six, seven, eight, or nine ones.
1.NBT.B.2.c	The numbers 10, 20, 30, 40, 50, 60, 70, 80, 90 refer to one, two, three, four, five, six, seven, eight, or nine tens (and 0 ones).
1.NBT.B.3	Compare two two-digit numbers based on meanings of the tens and ones digits, recording the results of comparisons with the symbols >, =, and <.
1.NBT.C.4	Add within 100, including adding a two-digit number and a one-digit number, and adding a two-digit number and a multiple of 10, using concrete models or drawings and strategies based on place value, properties of operations, and/or the relationship between addition and subtraction; relate the strategy to a written method and explain the reasoning used. Understand that in adding two-digit numbers, one adds tens and tens, ones and ones; and sometimes it is necessary to compose a ten.
1.NBT.C.5	Given a two-digit number, mentally find 10 more or 10 less than the number, without having to count; explain the reasoning used.
1.NBT.C.6	Subtract multiples of 10 in the range 10–90 from multiples of 10 in the range 10–90 (positive or zero differences), using concrete models or drawings and strategies based on place value, properties of operations, and/or the relationship between addition and subtraction; relate the strategy to a written method and explain the reasoning used.

(continued)

KIT MATERIALS
- *Make a Splash 120 Mat Floor Game*: 1.NBT.A.1, 1.NBT.C.4, 1.NBT.C.5, 1.NBT.C.6
- *Ten-Frame Trains*: 1.NBT.B.2.a, 1.NBT.B.2.b, 1.NBT.B.3, 1.NBT.C.4, 1.NBT.C.5, 1.NBT.C.6
- *Working with Ten-Frames*: 1.NBT.B.2.b, 1.NBT.C.6
- *Unifix Cubes*: 1.NBT.B.2.a, 1.NBT.B.2.b, 1.NBT.B.2.c, 1.NBT.B.3, 1.NBT.C.4, 1.NBT.C.6
- *Mathematics with Unifix Cubes*: 1.NBT.B.3, 1.NBT.C.4
- *Thinking Mats*: 1.NBT.B.2.c, 1.NBT.B.3, 1.NBT.C.4, 1.NBT.C.6
- *120 Number Mats*: 1.NBT.A.1, 1.NBT.B.2.c, 1.NBT.C.4, 1.NBT.C.6
- *Write-on/Wipe-off Crayons*: 1.NBT.A.1, 1.NBT.B.2.c, 1.NBT.C.4, 1.NBT.C.6

CLASSROOM MATERIALS AND ACTIVITIES
- Pennies and dimes
- Popsicle sticks
- Base ten blocks

TIP FOR GENERALIZATION
Create a "Number of the Day" bulletin board or center. Each day, identify the Number of the Day. Have students identify another way to write it. For example, if the number is "Fourteen," the student can write "14," draw fourteen dots, write "16 – 2," etc. Include other pieces of information for the student to fill in, such as "10 less = ____," "10 more = ____," a place value table, or circling whether the number is odd or even.

Number and Operations in Base Ten
Extend the counting sequence
1.NBT.A.1

STUDENT: _____

1.NBT.A.1 Count to 120, starting at any number less than 120. In this range, read and write numerals and represent a number of objects with a written numeral.

Materials: *Make a Splash 120 Mat Floor Game, 120 Number Mats, Write-on/Wipe-off Crayons*

Teaching Procedure: Place the *Make a Splash 120 Mat Floor Game* in view of all students. Set aside the Square Frames from the game. After your students have mastered counting from 1 to 120, place the square frame on a number on the mat, and tell students to count starting from that number. For example, you might place the square frame on the 57, then count to 120 from there. For students who are struggling with this skill, you may want to cover a portion of the mat and work with a small amount of numbers.

"Let's count." "Start with 81 and count to 120." "Can you count from here?"

TARGET	INTRODUCED	MASTERED	GENERALIZATION PROBE	
Independently counts from 1 to 20				
With prompting and support, counts to 20 starting at any number less than 20				
Independently counts to 20 starting at any number less than 20				
Independently counts from 1 to 50				
With prompting and support, counts to 50 starting at any number less than 50				
Independently counts to 50 starting at any number less than 50				
Independently counts from 1 to 120				
With prompting and support, counts to 120 starting at any number less than 120				
Independently counts to 120 starting at any number less than 120				
Add additional targets				

⚠ **If your student has not met the prerequisite skills for this standard, drill down to K.CC.A.1, K.CC.A.2, K.NBT.A.1.**

 Procedure and Data Collection: Run 10–20 trials per session with a **Y** or **N** per trial. Graph the overall percentage of the number correct on the Per Opportunity Graph.

Mastery Criterion: 80% correct across three consecutive sessions with two different instructors.

Number and Operations in Base Ten
Understand place value
1.NBT.B.2: 1.NBT.B.2.a, 1.NBT.B.2.b, 1.NBT.B.2.c
1.NBT.B.3

STUDENT: _____

1.NBT.B.2* Understand that the two digits of a two-digit number represent amounts of tens and ones. Understand the following as special cases: 1.NBT.B.2.a, 1.NBT.B.2.b, 1.NBT.B.2.c

This standard is divided into three more specified standards: 1.NBT.B.2.a, 1.NBT.B.2.b, and 1.NBT.B.2.c. Once these three standards have been met, 1.NBT.B.2 is considered mastered.

1.NBT.B.2.a 10 can be thought of as a bundle of ten ones—called a "ten."

Materials: *Unifix Cubes, Ten-Frame Trains*

Teaching Procedure: Prior to the lesson, prepare several materials that are stackable or attachable (such as paperclips, magnet tiles, or blocks), as well as the *Unifix Cubes* and *Ten-Frame Trains*. Model for students how to "bundle a ten" or make a "ten-stick." Provide several examples and non-examples of tens and ask students "Can I bundle these?" For example, count out ten *Unifix Cubes* and ask if they can be bundled. When students say "yes" show them how to connect them as a bundle. Then count out eight *Unifix Cubes* and ask if they can be bundled. After providing several examples and non-examples, allow students to practice on their own with several different materials.

"Can these be bundled?" "Is this a ten?" "Show me a ten-stick."

TARGET	INTRODUCED	MASTERED	GENERALIZATION PROBE	
With prompting and support, counts and identifies a group of 10 objects as a "ten"				
Independently counts and identifies a group of 10 objects as a "ten"				
With prompting and support, counts and bundles a group of 10 objects as a "ten"				
Independently counts and bundles a group of 10 objects as a "ten"				
With prompting and support, demonstrates how a "ten" is made up of ten ones				
Independently demonstrates how a "ten" is made up of ten ones				
Add additional target				

If your student has not met the prerequisite skills for this standard, drill down to K.NBT.A.1.

Procedure and Data Collection: Run 10–20 trials per session with a **Y** or **N** per trial. Graph the overall percentage of the number correct on the Per Opportunity Graph.

Mastery Criterion: 80% correct across three consecutive sessions with two different instructors.

Number and Operations in Base Ten
Understand place value
**1.NBT.B.2: 1.NBT.B.2.a, 1.NBT.B.2.b, 1.NBT.B.2.c
1.NBT.B.3**

STUDENT: _____

1.NBT.B.2*

Understand that the two digits of a two-digit number represent amounts of tens and ones. Understand the following as special cases: 1.NBT.B.2.a, 1.NBT.B.2.b, 1.NBT.B.2.c

*This standard is divided into three more specified standards: 1.NBT.B.2.a, 1.NBT.B.2.b, and 1.NBT.B.2.c.
Once these three standards have been met, 1.NBT.B.2 is considered mastered.*

1.NBT.B.2.b

The numbers from 11 to 19 are composed of a ten and one, two, three, four, five, six, seven, eight, or nine ones.

Materials: *Ten-Frame Trains, Unifix Cubes, Working with Ten-Frames,* Index Cards (not included in kit)

Teaching Procedure: Prior to the lesson, provide two *Ten-Frame Trains* to each pair of students as well as flashcards with the numbers 11 through 19 written on them. Model for students how to look at a flashcard, use the *Unifix Cubes* to represent that number in the *Ten-Frame Trains*, then identify what that number is composed of. For example, you draw the number 13, fill one Ten-Frame Train with ten cubes, and the second train with three more cubes to make 13. Then state, "Thirteen is composed of one ten and three ones." Provide several examples and then allow students to practice on their own.

"How do you make fourteen?" "What is an eleven composed of?" "What number is made up of one ten and five ones?"

TARGET	INTRODUCED	MASTERED	GENERALIZATION PROBE
With prompting and support, illustrates what numbers compose the numbers 11 to 19 with the use of manipulatives or drawings			
Independently illustrates what numbers compose the numbers 11 to 19 with the use of manipulatives or drawings			
With prompting and support, states what numbers compose the numbers 11 to 19 when provided with a visual example			
Independently states what numbers compose the numbers 11 to 19 when provided with a visual example			
With prompting and support, states what numbers compose the numbers 11 to 19 when provided the number verbally			
Independently states what numbers compose the numbers 11 to 19 when provided the number verbally			

(continued)

Number and Operations in Base Ten
Understand place value
1.NBT.B.2: 1.NBT.B.2.a, 1.NBT.B.2.b, 1.NBT.B.2.c
1.NBT.B.3

STUDENT: _____

(1.NBT.B.2.b page 2)

With prompting and support, provides the correct response when asked what number is made from one ten and x number of ones				
Independently provides the correct response when asked what number is made from one ten and x number of ones				
Add additional targets				

If your student has not met the prerequisite skills for this standard, drill down to K.CC.B.5, K.NBT.A.1.

Procedure and Data Collection: Run 10–20 trials per session with a **Y** or **N** per trial. Graph the overall percentage of the number correct on the Per Opportunity Graph.

Mastery Criterion: 80% correct across three consecutive sessions with two different instructors.

Number and Operations in Base Ten
Understand place value
**1.NBT.B.2: 1.NBT.B.2.a, 1.NBT.B.2.b, 1.NBT.B.2.c
1.NBT.B.3**

STUDENT: _____

1.NBT.B.2*

Understand that the two digits of a two-digit number represent amounts of tens and ones. Understand the following as special cases: 1.NBT.B.2.a, 1.NBT.B.2.b, 1.NBT.B.2.c

This standard is divided into three more specified standards: 1.NBT.B.2.a, 1.NBT.B.2.b, and 1.NBT.B.2.c. Once these three standards have been met, 1.NBT.B.2 is considered mastered.

1.NBT.B.2.c

The numbers 10, 20, 30, 40, 50, 60, 70, 80, 90 refer to one, two, three, four, five, six, seven, eight, or nine tens (and 0 ones).

Materials: *Unifix Cubes, 120 Number Mats, Write-on/Wipe-off Crayons, Thinking Mats*

Teaching Procedure: Place many *Unifix Cubes* within reach of your students. Ask each student to make a "ten" or a "ten-stick." Once all students have completed at least one ten, ask students, "How many tens do we have all together?" After students have responded, put some ten-sticks down, then hold up a smaller amount and ask, "How many tens do I have now?" Next, give each student a *120 Number Mat*. Point to the number 60 and ask "How many tens make 60?" Then, model placing a ten-stick on each ten until you get to 60, stating the number as you place each ten-stick on the mat. "Ten, twenty, thirty, forty, fifty, sixty. Let's count the tens: 1, 2, 3, 4, 5, 6. Sixty has *six* tens." Point out to students that 60 has six tens and it has a '6' in the tens place. Next, say, "Let's find out how many tens are in 20." Help students use the same process you demonstrated. Provide more practice as necessary. If students are mastering the skill with the use of the *Unifix Cubes*, challenge them to find the answer without using the ten-sticks.

"How many tens are in 60?" "I have nine tens. How many ones is that?" "How many tens make 30?"

TARGET	INTRODUCED	MASTERED	GENERALIZATION PROBE
With prompting and support, uses manipulatives to determine the number of tens in 10, 20, 30, 40, 50, 60, 70, 80, and 90 on 80% of trials			
Independently uses manipulatives to determine the number of tens in 10, 20, 30, 40, 50, 60, 70, 80, and 90 on 80% of trials			
With prompting and support, counts the number of ten-sticks and identifies the total number (i.e., counts eight ten-sticks and states that it makes 80)			
Independently counts the number of ten-sticks and identifies the total number (i.e., counts eight ten-sticks and states that it makes 80)			
With prompting and support, determines the number of tens in 10, 20, 30, 40, 50, 60, 70, 80, and 90 on 80% of trials without the use of manipulatives			
Independently determines the number of tens in 10, 20, 30, 40, 50, 60, 70, 80, and 90 on 80% of trials without the use of manipulatives			

(continued)

Number and Operations in Base Ten
Understand place value
1.NBT.B.2: 1.NBT.B.2.a, 1.NBT.B.2.b, 1.NBT.B.2.c
1.NBT.B.3

STUDENT: _____

(1.NBT.B.2.c page 2)

Add additional targets				

If your student has not met the prerequisite skills for this standard, drill down to K.NBT.A.1.

Procedure and Data Collection: Run 10–20 trials per session with a **Y** or **N** per trial.
Graph the overall percentage of the number correct on the Per Opportunity Graph.

Mastery Criterion: 80% correct across three consecutive sessions with two different instructors.

Number and Operations in Base Ten
Understand place value
1.NBT.B.2: 1.NBT.B.2.a, 1.NBT.B.2.b, 1.NBT.B.2.c
1.NBT.B.3

STUDENT: _____

1.NBT.B.3

Compare two two-digit numbers based on meanings of the tens and ones digits, recording the results of comparisons with the symbols >, =, and <.

Materials: *Mathematics with Unifix Cubes, Unifix Cubes, Thinking Mats, Ten-Frame Trains*

Teaching Procedure: Prior to the lesson, make a copy of the Unifix "1–10 Stair" on Page 14 from *Mathematics with Unifix Cubes* for each student. Provide each student with 20 *Unifix Cubes*. Call out two numbers (such as 3 and 7). Have students put together *Unifix Cubes* for each number, then place them in the correct space on the 1–10 Stair. Ask students to compare the two numbers, providing questions such as "Which is bigger?" "Which number is less?" Have students remove the *Unifix Cubes*, then provide a set of two new numbers. Provide several opportunities for practice and allow individual students to select the two numbers for comparison as well.

"Which number is greater?" "Compare these two numbers." "What symbol makes the number sentence true?"

TARGET	INTRODUCED	MASTERED	GENERALIZATION PROBE
With prompting and support, compares digits between 1 and 5 by identifying which number is "bigger," "smaller," or "the same"			
Independently compares digits between 1 and 5 by identifying which number is "bigger," "smaller," or "the same"			
With prompting and support, compares digits between 1 and 5 by identifying which number is "greater than," "less than," or "equal"			
Independently compares digits between 1 and 5 by identifying which number is "greater than," "less than," or "equal"			
With prompting and support, compares digits between 1 and 5 by identifying which number is "greater than," "less than," or "equal" and records the results with the symbols >, =, and <			
Independently compares digits between 1 and 5 by identifying which number is "greater than," "less than," or "equal" and records the results with the symbols >, =, and <			
With prompting and support, compares digits between 1 and 20 by identifying which number is "greater than," "less than," or "equal" and records the results with the symbols >, =, and <			

(continued)

Number and Operations in Base Ten
Understand place value
**1.NBT.B.2: 1.NBT.B.2.a, 1.NBT.B.2.b, 1.NBT.B.2.c
1.NBT.B.3**

STUDENT: _____

(1.NBT.B.3 page 2)

Independently compares digits between 1 and 20 by identifying which number is "greater than," "less than," or "equal" and records the results with the symbols >, =, or <				
With prompting and support, compares digits between 1 and 50 by identifying which number is "greater than," "less than," or "equal" and records the results with the symbols >, =, or <				
Independently compares digits between 1 and 50 by identifying which number is "greater than," "less than," or "equal" and records the results with the symbols >, =, or <				
With prompting and support, compares digits between 1 and 99 by identifying which number is "greater than," "less than," or "equal" and records the results with the symbols >, =, or <				
Independently compares digits between 1 and 99 by identifying which number is "greater than," "less than," or "equal" and records the results with the symbols >, =, or <				
Add additional targets				

If your student has not met the prerequisite skills for this standard, drill down to K.CC.C.7, K.NBT.A.1.

Procedure and Data Collection: Run 10–20 trials per session with a **Y** or **N** per trial.
Graph the overall percentage of the number correct on the Per Opportunity Graph.

Mastery Criterion: 80% correct across three consecutive sessions with two different instructors.

Number and Operations in Base Ten
Use place value understanding and properties
of operations to add and subtract
1.NBT.C.4, 1.NBT.C.5, 1.NBT.C.6

STUDENT: _____

1.NBT.C.4 Add within 100, including adding a two-digit number and a one-digit number, and adding a two-digit number and a multiple of 10, using concrete models or drawings and strategies based on place value, properties of operations, and/or the relationship between addition and subtraction; relate the strategy to a written method and explain the reasoning used. Understand that in adding two-digit numbers, one adds tens and tens, ones and ones; and sometimes it is necessary to compose a ten.

Materials: *Unifix Cubes, Mathematics with Unifix Cubes, 120 Number Mats, Write-on/Wipe-off Crayons, Make a Splash 120 Mat Floor Game, Ten-Frame Trains, Thinking Mats,* Index cards, Timer (not included in kit)

Teaching Procedure: Prior to the lesson, prepare several "stations" with different manipulatives and drawing materials for demonstrating how to add. Then, prepare several index cards with a different addition problem on each. (You can easily differentiate this lesson by preparing groups of colored index cards based on skill level and assign each student to a specific color or group.) Demonstrate for students how to pick up an index card, read the problem aloud, and then use the manipulatives at the station to find the answer. Use an audible timer to signal when it's time to move to another station, and allow students plenty of time to explore addition problems with manipulatives and drawings at each station.

"Let's add." "Can you figure out how many there are all together?" "Tell me how you did that."

TARGET	INTRODUCED	MASTERED	GENERALIZATION PROBE
With the use of manipulatives and/or drawings, adds a one-digit number to a one-digit number			
Independently adds a one-digit number to a one-digit number			
With the use of manipulatives and/or drawings, adds a two-digit number to a one-digit number for numbers within 25			
With the use of manipulatives and/or drawings, adds a two-digit number to a one-digit number for numbers within 50			
With the use of manipulatives and/or drawings, adds a two-digit number to a one-digit number for numbers within 100			
With the use of manipulatives and/or drawings, adds a two-digit number to a multiple of 10 for numbers within 100			
When adding using manipulatives and/or drawings, provides explanation of the strategy used, including information related to place value, with prompting and support			

(continued)

Number and Operations in Base Ten
Use place value understanding and properties
of operations to add and subtract
1.NBT.C.4, 1.NBT.C.5, 1.NBT.C.6

STUDENT: _____

(1.NBT.C.4 page 2)

When adding using manipulatives and/or drawings, independently provides explanation of the strategy used, including information related to place value				
When adding using manipulatives and/or drawings, provides explanation of the strategy used, including information related to properties of operations, with prompting and support				
When adding using manipulatives and/or drawings, independently provides explanation of the strategy used, including information related to properties of operations				
When adding using manipulatives and/or drawings, provides explanation of the strategy used, including information related to the relationship between addition and subtraction, with prompting and support				
When adding using manipulatives and/or drawings, independently provides explanation of the strategy used, including information related to the relationship between addition and subtraction				
With prompting and support, tells or shows how an addition problem should be written				
Independently tells or shows how an addition problem should be written				
Add additional targets				

 If your student has not met the prerequisite skills for this standard, drill down to **K.OA.A.1, K.NBT.A.1.**

 Procedure and Data Collection: Run 10–20 trials per session with a **Y** or **N** per trial. Graph the overall percentage of the number correct on the Per Opportunity Graph.

Mastery Criterion: 80% correct across three consecutive sessions with two different instructors.

Number and Operations in Base Ten
Use place value understanding and properties
of operations to add and subtract
1.NBT.C.4, 1.NBT.C.5, 1.NBT.C.6

1.NBT.C.5

Given a two-digit number, mentally find 10 more or 10 less than the number, without having to count; explain the reasoning used.

Materials: *Make a Splash 120 Mat Floor Game, Ten-Frame Trains*

Teaching Procedure: Prior to the lesson, prepare the *Make a Splash 120 Mat Floor Game*, utilizing the four T-shaped "more/less than pieces," and the inflatable cube with +10, –10, +1, and –1. Name a number, then model for students how to use the T-shape to find ten more and ten less than the number named. Give students many opportunities to practice using the T-shape. Then, introduce the inflatable cube and have students take turns rolling the dice to find ten more or ten less than a named number.

"What is 10 less than 24?" "Can you find the number that is 10 more than 73?"

TARGET	INTRODUCED	MASTERED	GENERALIZATION PROBE	
With prompting and visual supports, identifies a number that is 10 more than a given two-digit number				
Independently utilizes visual supports and identifies a number that is 10 more than a given two-digit number				
Independently identifies a number that is 10 more than a given two-digit number without the use of visual supports or counting				
With prompting and visual supports, identifies a number that is 10 less than a given two-digit number				
Independently utilizes visual supports and identifies a number that is 10 less than a given two-digit number				
Independently identifies a number that is 10 less than a given two-digit number without the use of visual supports or counting				
Independently responds to a random mix of questions requiring identification of 10 more or 10 less than a two-digit number without the use of visual supports or counting				
With prompting and support, explains the reasoning used for determining the correct response				
Independently explains the reasoning used for determining the correct response				

(continued)

Number and Operations in Base Ten
Use place value understanding and properties
of operations to add and subtract
1.NBT.C.4, 1.NBT.C.5, 1.NBT.C.6

STUDENT: _____

(1.NBT.C.5 page 2)

Add additional targets				

⚠ **If your student has not met the prerequisite skills for this standard, drill down to K.NBT.A.1.**

 Procedure and Data Collection: Run 10–20 trials per session with a **Y** or **N** per trial.
Graph the overall percentage of the number correct on the Per Opportunity Graph.

Mastery Criterion: 80% correct across three consecutive sessions with two different instructors.

Number and Operations in Base Ten
Use place value understanding and properties
of operations to add and subtract
1.NBT.C.4, 1.NBT.C.5, 1.NBT.C.6

STUDENT: _____

1.NBT.C.6

Subtract multiples of 10 in the range 10–90 from multiples of 10 in the range 10–90 (positive or zero differences), using concrete models or drawings and strategies based on place value, properties of operations, and/or the relationship between addition and subtraction; relate the strategy to a written method and explain the reasoning used.

Materials: *Working with Ten-Frames, 120 Number Mats,* Write-on/Wipe-off Crayons, Unifix Cubes, *Make a Splash 120 Mat Floor Game, Ten-Frame Trains, Thinking Mats*

Teaching Procedure: Prior to the lesson, reproduce multiple copies of the "Tic-Tac-Toe Game" Mat on page 167 of *Working with Ten-Frames,* and copy and cut the Tic-Tac-Toe Problem Cards. Then, provide each student with a *120 Number Mat.* You may want to divide the class into teams for this activity, but you can also allow them to play individually. Demonstrate for students how to use the *120 Number Mat* to solve subtractions problems within 10–90 from multiples of 10 (e.g., 80–20 or 50–10). Tell students they are going to play Tic-Tac-Toe Subtraction. The first person to get three in a row wins!

"What is 70 minus 40?" "Can you subtract?" "Let's subtract." "Tell me how you figured that out."

TARGET	INTRODUCED	MASTERED	GENERALIZATION PROBE	
With the use of manipulatives and/or drawings, subtracts a one-digit number from a one-digit number				
Independently subtracts a one-digit number from a one-digit number				
With the use of manipulatives and/or drawings, subtracts a multiple of 10 from a multiple of 10 within the range of 10–50				
With the use of manipulatives and/or drawings, subtracts a multiple of 10 from a multiple of 10 within the range of 10–90				
With prompting and support, provides explanation of the strategy used when subtracting using manipulatives and/or drawings, including information related to place value				
Independently provides explanation of the strategy used when subtracting using manipulatives and/or drawings, including information related to place value				
With prompting and support, provides explanation of the strategy used when subtracting using manipulatives and/or drawings, including information related to properties of operations				

(continued)

Number and Operations in Base Ten
Use place value understanding and properties
of operations to add and subtract
1.NBT.C.4, 1.NBT.C.5, 1.NBT.C.6

STUDENT: _____

(1.NBT.C.6 page 2)

Independently provides explanation of the strategy used when subtracting using manipulatives and/or drawings, including information related to properties of operations				
With prompting and support, provides explanation of the strategy used when subtracting using manipulatives and/or drawings, including information related to the relationship between addition and subtraction				
Independently provides explanation of the strategy used when subtracting using manipulatives and/or drawings, including information related to the relationship between addition and subtraction				
With prompting and support, tells or shows how a subtraction problem should be written				
Independently tells or shows how a subtraction problem should be written				
Add additional targets				

 If your student has not met the prerequisite skills for this standard, drill down to K.OA.A.1, K.OA.A.2, K.NBT.A.1.

 Procedure and Data Collection: Run 10–20 trials per session with a **Y** or **N** per trial.
Graph the overall percentage of the number correct on the Per Opportunity Graph.

Mastery Criterion: 80% correct across three consecutive sessions with two different instructors.

MEASUREMENT AND DATA OVERVIEW

· Measure lengths indirectly and by iterating length units
· Tell and write time
· Represent and interpret data

CCSS CODE	STANDARD
1.MD.A.1	Order three objects by length; compare the lengths of two objects indirectly by using a third object.
1.MD.A.2	Express the length of an object as a whole number of length units, by laying multiple copies of a shorter object (the length unit) end to end; understand that the length measurement of an object is the number of same-size length units that span it with no gaps or overlaps. Limit to contexts where the object being measured is spanned by a whole number of length units with no gaps or overlaps.
1.MD.B.3	Tell and write time in hours and half-hours using analog and digital clocks.
1.MD.C.4	Organize, represent, and interpret data with up to three categories; ask and answer questions about the total number of data points, how many in each category, and how many more or less are in one category than in another.

KIT MATERIALS

· *Unifix Cubes*: 1.MD.A.1, 1.MD.A.2, 1.MD.C.4
· *Mathematics with Unifix Cubes:* 1.MD.A.1, 1.MD.A.2, 1.MD.C.4
· *Thinking Mats*: 1.MD.A.1, 1.MD.A.2, 1.MD.B.3, 1.MD.C.4
· *Write-on/Wipe-off Clock Boards*: 1.MD.B.3
· *Write-on/Wipe-off Crayons*: 1.MD.B.3

CLASSROOM MATERIALS AND ACTIVITIES

· Clocks in the natural environment
· Height measurements of peers
· Rulers, measuring tapes, yard sticks

TIP FOR GENERALIZATION

Prepare three containers for each student: one with paperclips, another with beans, and a final with toothpicks. Tell students you are going to use these items as units of measurement. Let each student select five objects to measure with each unit in their container. For example, a student might select a notebook, and then record its length by the number of units of paperclips, beans and toothpicks. Lead the class in a discussion of why they found different measurements with each item.

1.MD.A.1 Order three objects by length; compare the lengths of two objects indirectly by using a third object.

Materials: *Unifix Cubes, Mathematics with Unifix Cubes, Thinking Mats*

Teaching Procedure: Provide each student with 10–12 *Unifix Cubes* of the same color (ideally, each student will have a different color). Model for students how to measure your hand using the *Unifix Cubes*. Then have each student create a stick of *Unifix Cubes* that is the length of his/her hand. If you have paraprofessional or assistant teachers, have them do so as well. Next, take your stick of cubes and the stick of one of your students, and model for students how to compare the two lengths. Have each student find a partner to compare with. Then, take your stick and the sticks of two other students and model for students how to put them in order by length. If there is additional time, repeat the activity with measurements of feet.

"Which object is the longest?" "Is this longer or shorter than that one?" "Can you compare the lengths of these two objects?" "Put them in order from shortest to longest."

TARGET	INTRODUCED	MASTERED	GENERALIZATION PROBE	
When provided with two objects and asked which is shorter, touches the shorter object				
When provided with two objects and asked which is longer, touches the longer object				
When provided with three objects and asked which is shortest, touches the shortest object				
When provided with three objects and asked which is longest, touches the longest object				
When provided with three objects and asked to put them in order from shortest to longest, arranges them correctly				
When provided with three objects and asked to put them in order from longest to shortest, arranges them correctly				
When provided with two objects and asked to compare them, labels "shorter" and "longer"				
When provided with three objects and asked to compare them, labels "shortest" and "longest"				
When provided with three objects and asked to compare them, uses language such as "shorter than" and "longer than" to compare their lengths				

(continued)

STUDENT: _____

(1.MD.A.1 page 2)

Add additional targets				

 If your student has not met the prerequisite skills for this standard, drill down to K.MD.A.1, K.MD.A.2.

 Procedure and Data Collection: Run 10–20 trials per session with a **Y** or **N** per trial. Graph the overall percentage of the number correct on the Per Opportunity Graph.

Mastery Criterion: 80% correct across three consecutive sessions with two different instructors.

1.MD.A.2 Express the length of an object as a whole number of length units, by laying multiple copies of a shorter object (the length unit) end to end; understand that the length measurement of an object is the number of same-size length units that span it with no gaps or overlaps. *Limit to contexts where the object being measured is spanned by a whole number of length units with no gaps or overlaps.*

Materials: *Mathematics with Unifix Cubes, Unifix Cubes*

Teaching Procedure: Prior to the lesson, reproduce page 83 of *Mathematics with Unfix Cubes* for each student, cut the measurement bars, and place them in an envelope for each student. Provide each student or group of students with 55 *Unifix Cubes*. Model how to attach the *Unifix Cubes* end to end in order to identify the number of *Unifix Cubes* it takes to measure an object. Tell students to take a bar out of their envelopes, then measure that bar using the cubes. When students have completed all the bars, challenge them to put the bars in order from shortest to longest.

"How long is the book?" "Show me how to measure that." "Tell me how you figured out the length."

TARGET	INTRODUCED	MASTERED	GENERALIZATION PROBE	
With prompting and support, measures an object by placing units end to end				
Independently measures an object by placing units end to end				
With prompting and support, measures an object and identifies the number of units that make up the length				
After measuring an object, independently identifies the number of units that make up the length				
With prompting and support, selects a unit of measurement that is comprised of same-size length units (e.g., when the teacher provides a selection of different items, the student selects paperclips as a unit of measurement to measure his/her foot)				
Independently selects a unit of measurement that is comprised of same-size length units (e.g., the student independently selects pennies as a unit of measurement to measure his/her foot)				
Add additional target				

 If your student has not met the prerequisite skills for this standard, drill down to K.CC.C.6.

 Procedure and Data Collection: Run 10–20 trials per session with a **Y** or **N** per trial. Graph the overall percentage of the number correct on the Per Opportunity Graph.

Mastery Criterion: 80% correct across three consecutive sessions with two different instructors.

STUDENT: _____

1.MD.B.3 Tell and write time in hours and half-hours using analog and digital clocks.

Materials: *Write-on/Wipe-off Clock Boards, Write-on/Wipe-off Crayons, Thinking Mats*

Teaching Procedure: Prior to the lesson, write times on each *Clock Board* with a wipe-away crayon. First introduce only times on the hour with a digital clock. Model for students how to read a digital clock by pointing to each digit as you read it aloud. Then place the *Clock Boards* in view of all students and ask them to point to the clock that says 5:00. Provide several opportunities to practice. Next, give each student a *Clock Board* and a wipe-away crayon. Name a time and have students write it on their clock board, then hold it up for you to see.

"What time is it?" "Which clock says four o'clock?" "Can you read this clock?"

TARGET	INTRODUCED	MASTERED	GENERALIZATION PROBE
With prompting and support, tells the time in hours on a digital clock			
Independently tells the time in hours on a digital clock			
With prompting and support, writes the time in hours on a digital clock			
Independently writes the time in hours on a digital clock			
With prompting and support, tells the time in hours on an analog clock			
Independently tells the time in hours on an analog clock			
With prompting and support, writes the time in hours on an analog clock			
Independently writes the time in hours on an analog clock			
With prompting and support, tells the time in half-hours on a digital clock			
Independently tells the time in half-hours on a digital clock			
With prompting and support, writes the time in half-hours on a digital clock			
Independently writes the time in half-hours on a digital clock			

(continued)

STUDENT: _____

With prompting and support, tells the time in half-hours on an analog clock				
Independently tells the time in half-hours on an analog clock				
With prompting and support, writes the time in half-hours on an analog clock				
Independently writes the time in half-hours on an analog clock				
With prompting and support, tells the time when hour and half-hour increments are shown				
Independently tells the time when hour and half-hour increments are shown				
Add additional targets				

If your student has not met the prerequisite skills for this standard, drill down to K.CC.A.1.

Procedure and Data Collection: Run 10–20 trials per session with a **Y** or **N** per trial.
Graph the overall percentage of the number correct on the Per Opportunity Graph.

Mastery Criterion: 80% correct across three consecutive sessions with two different instructors.

STUDENT: _____

1.MD.C.4 Organize, represent, and interpret data with up to three categories; ask and answer questions about the total number of data points, how many in each category, and how many more or less are in one category than in another.

Materials: *Thinking Mats,* Unifix Cubes, *Mathematics with Unifix Cubes*

Teaching Procedure: Prior to the lesson, remove the "Mark's Mess" folder from the *Thinking Mats*. Place it so it is within view of all students. Select a student to choose an object to find in Mark's room, and then place that object card on the "object" box of the mat. Model for students how to count and tally that object. For example, if the student selected "shoes," model for students how to count the shoes in the room and make the tally marks. Repeat this process two more times so students can compare the tallied totals of three objects. Depending upon your students' skill levels, you can also represent the data using a bar graph.

"How can we organize this information?" "Can you draw a bar graph to show me the information?" "Let's make a graph."

TARGET	INTRODUCED	MASTERED	GENERALIZATION PROBE	
With prompting and support, tallies counted data for one category				
Independently tallies counted data for one category				
With prompting and support, tallies counted data for two categories				
Independently tallies counted data for two categories				
With prompting and support, tallies counted data for three categories				
Independently tallies counted data for three categories				
With prompting and support, converts tallied data to a bar graph				
Independently converts tallied data to a bar graph				
Add additional target				

If your student has not met the prerequisite skills for this standard, drill down to K.MD.B.3.

Procedure and Data Collection: Run 10–20 trials per session with a **Y** or **N** per trial. Graph the overall percentage of the number correct on the Per Opportunity Graph.

Mastery Criterion: 80% correct across three consecutive sessions with two different instructors.

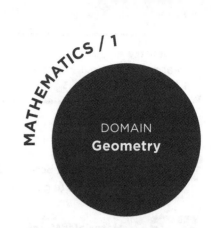

DOMAIN
Geometry

GEOMETRY OVERVIEW

· Reason with shapes and their attributes

CCSS CODE	STANDARD
1.G.A.1	Distinguish between defining attributes (e.g., triangles are closed and three-sided) versus non-defining attributes (e.g., color, orientation, overall size); build and draw shapes to possess defining attributes.
1.G.A.2	Compose two-dimensional shapes (rectangles, squares, trapezoids, triangles, half-circles, and quarter-circles) or three-dimensional shapes (cubes, right rectangular prisms, right circular cones, and right circular cylinders) to create a composite shape, and compose new shapes from the composite shape.[1]
1.G.A.3	Partition circles and rectangles into two and four equal shares, describe the shares using the words halves, fourths, and quarters, and use the phrases half of, fourth of, and quarter of. Describe the whole as two of, or four of the shares. Understand for these examples that decomposing into more equal shares creates smaller shares.

[1] *Students should apply the principle of transitivity of measurement to make indirect comparisons, but they need not use this technical term.*

KIT MATERIALS

· *Match It! Shape Shuffle*: 1.G.A.1, 1.G.A.2, 1.G.A.3
· *Thinking Mats*: 1.G.A.1, 1.G.A.2, 1.G.A.3

CLASSROOM MATERIALS AND ACTIVITIES

· Teacher or student-created shapes
· Tangrams
· Shape puzzles
· Modeling materials: clay, straw, toothpicks, etc.

TIP FOR GENERALIZATION

During a community walk, do a Geometry Scavenger Hunt. Provide each student with one shape. That student must find as many examples of that shape in the neighborhood and share those examples with the class. You may want to bring along digital cameras so students can photograph and share (through oral or written communication) the shapes they found on the Scavenger Hunt.

STUDENT: _____

1.G.A.1 Distinguish between defining attributes (e.g., triangles are closed and three-sided) versus non-defining attributes (e.g., color, orientation, overall size); build and draw shapes to possess defining attributes.

Materials: *Match It! Shape Shuffle, Thinking Mats*

Teaching Procedure: Place several examples of a square on the table in view of all students. Ask students to name the shape. On the dry-erase board or on a poster, write the name of the shape at the top. Then, ask students to tell you about the shape. Write the attributes for that shape on the board or poster. For example, if you are showing a square, the attributes would be "closed," "four-sided," and "all sides are equal." After identifying all of the defining attributes, place several examples and non-examples of the shape from the *Match It! Shape Shuffle* on the table. Have students identify whether each shape is or is not a square and explain why using the attributes you've discussed.

"How do you know this is a triangle?" "What is the difference between a triangle and a square?" "Name this shape."

TARGET	INTRODUCED	MASTERED	GENERALIZATION PROBE	
With prompting and support, identifies the name of a shape for at least three shapes				
Independently identifies the name of a shape for at least three shapes				
With prompting and support, identifies the name of a shape for at least eight shapes				
Independently identifies the name of a shape for at least eight shapes				
With prompting and support, identifies one defining attribute for at least three shapes				
Independently identifies one defining attribute for at least three shapes				
With prompting and support, identifies one defining attribute for at least eight shapes				
Independently identifies one defining attribute for at least eight shapes				
With prompting and support, identifies two or more defining attributes for at least eight shapes				
Independently identifies two or more defining attributes for at least eight shapes				

(continued)

STUDENT: _____

(1.G.A.1 page 2)

With prompting and support, draws or constructs a named shape according to its defining attributes for at least three shapes				
Independently draws or constructs a named shape according to its defining attributes for at least three shapes				
With prompting and support, draws or constructs a named shape according to its defining attributes for at least eight shapes				
Independently draws or constructs a named shape according to its defining attributes for at least eight shapes				
Add additional targets				

 If your student has not met the prerequisite skills for this standard, drill down to K.G.A.1, K.G.A.2.

 Procedure and Data Collection: Run 10–20 trials per session with a **Y** or **N** per trial.
Graph the overall percentage of the number correct on the Per Opportunity Graph.

Mastery Criterion: 80% correct across three consecutive sessions with two different instructors.

STUDENT: _____

1.G.A.2 Compose two-dimensional shapes (rectangles, squares, trapezoids, triangles, half-circles, and quarter-circles) or three-dimensional shapes (cubes, right rectangular prisms, right circular cones, and right circular cylinders) to create a composite shape, and compose new shapes from the composite shape.[1]

[1] Students should apply the principle of transitivity of measurement to make indirect comparisons, but they need not use this technical term.

Materials: *Thinking Mats, Match It! Shape Shuffle*

Teaching Procedure: Prior to the lesson, remove the "Treasure Map" folder from the *Thinking Mats*. Place it so it is within view of all students. Tell students you have to put the treasure map together, but the only way the map will fit together is if you can compose the five shapes correctly. Have students take turns placing the pieces on the treasure map board and describing what they've done. Upon completion of all the shapes, reveal the treasure which should be a reinforcer the whole class enjoys such as a listening to a specific song or participating in a movement activity.

"Can you use these shapes to compose a trapezoid?" "Let's make a cone." "How can we make a half-circle?"

TARGET	INTRODUCED	MASTERED	GENERALIZATION PROBE	
With prompting and support, composes at least two two-dimensional shapes				
Independently composes at least two two-dimensional shapes				
With prompting and support, composes at least five two-dimensional shapes				
Independently composes at least five two-dimensional shapes				
With prompting and support, composes six or more two-dimensional shapes				
Independently composes six or more two-dimensional shapes				
With prompting and support, composes at least two three-dimensional shapes				
Independently composes at least two three-dimensional shapes				
With prompting and support, composes at least five three-dimensional shapes				
Independently composes at least five three-dimensional shapes				

(continued)

STUDENT: _____

(1.G.A.2 page 2)

With prompting and support, composes six or more three-dimensional shapes				
Independently composes six or more three-dimensional shapes				
Add additional targets				

If your student has not met the prerequisite skills for this standard, drill down to K.G.A.3, K.G.B.4, K.G.B.5.

Procedure and Data Collection: Run 10–20 trials per session with a **Y** or **N** per trial. Graph the overall percentage of the number correct on the Per Opportunity Graph.

Mastery Criterion: 80% correct across three consecutive sessions with two different instructors.

STUDENT: _____

1.G.A.3 Partition circles and rectangles into two and four equal shares, describe the shares using the words *halves*, *fourths*, and *quarters*, and use the phrases *half of*, *fourth of*, and *quarter of*. Describe the whole as two of, or four of the shares. Understand for these examples that decomposing into more equal shares creates smaller shares.

Materials: *Match It! Shape Shuffle, Thinking Mats*

Teaching Procedure: Prior to the lesson, laminate several large, colored circles and rectangles. Cut some of them into two equal shares and others into four equal shares. Allow students to explore putting them together to make the whole, and taking them apart to make shares. For some students, it may be beneficial to have a poster board to serve as a base and use Velcro on the backs of the cut-up shapes to easily put together the whole. Hold up one share of a circle divided into two parts and say, "This is half of a circle. Can you find half of a circle in your shapes?" Provide several examples using the language "half of" or "halves" and allow students to find examples with their own shapes.

"What is this called?" "Can you show me half of a rectangle?" "Give me both halves of the red circle."

TARGET	INTRODUCED	MASTERED	GENERALIZATION PROBE
When provided with a sample, points to half of a circle or rectangle			
Independently labels one of two shares as "half of" the shape			
Independently labels the two shares as "halves" of the circle or rectangle			
When provided with a sample, points to a fourth of a circle or rectangle			
Independently labels one of four shares as "a fourth of" the shape			
Independently labels the four shares as "fourths" of the circle or rectangle			
When provided with a sample, points to a quarter of a circle or rectangle			
Independently labels one of four shares as "a quarter of" the shape			
Independently labels the four shares as "quarters" of the circle or rectangle			

(continued)

STUDENT: _____

(1.G.A.3 page 2)

Add additional targets				

 If your student has not met the prerequisite skills for this standard, drill down to **K.G.A.1, K.G.A.2, K.G.B.6.**

 Procedure and Data Collection: Run 10–20 trials per session with a **Y** or **N** per trial. Graph the overall percentage of the number correct on the Per Opportunity Graph.

Mastery Criterion: 80% correct across three consecutive sessions with two different instructors.

APPENDIX

A

Preference Assessment

Preference Assessment

Conducting a preference assessment for each student should be one of the first things you do. Having a clear understanding of what items and activities are highly motivating for your student will provide opportunities to reinforce for correct responses and adaptive behavior.

To conduct a preference assessment, place many toys and objects around a room and watch how the student interacts with them for about 20-30 minutes. If you have a student with poor scanning skills, you can present items two at a time and see what the learner reaches for.

You will make several presentations of items to the student, arranging them in different groupings. As you are observing, place tally marks in the charts below to easily recognize patterns. When you have completed the assessment, fill in the final page to have a comprehensive list of reinforcing items and activities.

VISUAL STIMULI				
STIMULUS	PICKED FIRST FROM ARRAY OF 3-5 ITEMS	INTERACTED WITH FOR ONE OR MORE MINUTES	INTERACTED WITH FOR FIVE OR MORE MINUTES	REQUESTED WHEN ITEM WAS NOT PRESENT OR OUT OF SIGHT
Light up toy				
Spinning toy (i.e., top)				
Jigsaw puzzle				
Stickers				

TACTILE STIMULI				
STIMULUS	PICKED FIRST FROM ARRAY OF 3-5 ITEMS	INTERACTED WITH FOR ONE OR MORE MINUTES	INTERACTED WITH FOR FIVE OR MORE MINUTES	REQUESTED WHEN ITEM WAS NOT PRESENT OR OUT OF SIGHT
Hugs				
Massage				
Vibrating items				
Unusual textures				

Preference Assessment

AUDITORY STIMULI				
STIMULUS	**PICKED FIRST FROM ARRAY OF 3-5 ITEMS**	**INTERACTED WITH FOR ONE OR MORE MINUTES**	**INTERACTED WITH FOR FIVE OR MORE MINUTES**	**REQUESTED WHEN ITEM WAS NOT PRESENT OR OUT OF SIGHT**
Music				
Playing instruments				
Teacher or parent singing				

MOVEMENT STIMULI				
STIMULUS	**PICKED FIRST FROM ARRAY OF 3-5 ITEMS**	**INTERACTED WITH FOR ONE OR MORE MINUTES**	**INTERACTED WITH FOR FIVE OR MORE MINUTES**	**REQUESTED WHEN ITEM WAS NOT PRESENT OR OUT OF SIGHT**
Running				
Jumping				
Spinning				

Preference Assessment

OLFACTORY STIMULI				
STIMULUS	**PICKED FIRST FROM ARRAY OF 3-5 ITEMS**	**INTERACTED WITH FOR ONE OR MORE MINUTES**	**INTERACTED WITH FOR FIVE OR MORE MINUTES**	**REQUESTED WHEN ITEM WAS NOT PRESENT OR OUT OF SIGHT**
Flowers				
Perfume				
Aroma from food				
Scratch & Sniff stickers				

GUSTATORY STIMULI				
STIMULUS	**PICKED FIRST FROM ARRAY OF 3-5 ITEMS**	**INTERACTED WITH FOR ONE OR MORE MINUTES**	**INTERACTED WITH FOR FIVE OR MORE MINUTES**	**REQUESTED WHEN ITEM WAS NOT PRESENT OR OUT OF SIGHT**
Pizza				
Crackers				
Chewing				
Salty food or snacks				

Preference Assessment

SOCIAL STIMULI				
STIMULUS	**PICKED FIRST FROM ARRAY OF 3-5 ITEMS**	**INTERACTED WITH FOR ONE OR MORE MINUTES**	**INTERACTED WITH FOR FIVE OR MORE MINUTES**	**REQUESTED WHEN ITEM WAS NOT PRESENT OR OUT OF SIGHT**
Smiles				
High fives				
Singing together				
Interactive games				
Conversation				

VESTIBULAR STIMULI				
STIMULUS	**PICKED FIRST FROM ARRAY OF 3-5 ITEMS**	**INTERACTED WITH FOR ONE OR MORE MINUTES**	**INTERACTED WITH FOR FIVE OR MORE MINUTES**	**REQUESTED WHEN ITEM WAS NOT PRESENT OR OUT OF SIGHT**
Riding a bike				
Rocking				
Swinging				
Trampoline				

Preference Assessment

ELECTRONIC/COMPUTER STIMULI – *List specific apps, computer games, and TV shows in the "Item" column*				
ITEM	PICKED FIRST FROM ARRAY OF 3–5 ITEMS	INTERACTED WITH FOR ONE OR MORE MINUTES	INTERACTED WITH FOR FIVE OR MORE MINUTES	REQUESTED WHEN ITEM WAS NOT PRESENT OR OUT OF SIGHT

Preference Assessment

List items in order from most tally marks recorded to least tally marks recorded.

1. _____
2. _____
3. _____
4. _____
5. _____
6. _____
7. _____
8. _____
9. _____
10. _____
11. _____
12. _____
13. _____
14. _____
15. _____

Parents report that the student is most interested in the items/activities below:

1. _____
2. _____
3. _____
4. _____
5. _____

APPENDIX

B

Encouraging Social Interactions
and Conversations

Encouraging Social Interactions and Conversations

MANDING

Manding (or making requests) is the cornerstone of all future communication. When working with students who are struggling with communication, you may have "manding sessions" in which your primary goal is to practice having the student mand or request preferred items and activities. However, there are many opportunities to practice manding throughout the school day. Below are some suggestions for mands you can teach. It should be noted that the student should be motivated to receive the item or engage in the activity that you are teaching him/her to request. For example,

if your student does not like washing his/her hands, you should not teach that as a mand.

For students who struggle with acquiring and using language, you should utilize the free downloads available at www.avbpress.com/vb-mapp. The Intraverbal Subset and 240 Word List are especially helpful in setting individualized, developmentally appropriate goals for your students who are not yet ready for grade-level standards.

SNACK TIME/LUNCH
"Juice"
Sign for "Cookie"
"Pour" (water or milk)
"Wash hands"

COMPUTER ACTIVITIES
Name of specific program/app
"Type"
"Turn on computer"
"Push play"

CIRCLE TIME
Name of favorite song
Raising hand (request for attention)
"Can I be the helper?"
"Get up"

PLAYGROUND
Pulling you towards swings
"Push"
"Throw"
"Ball"

MATH MANIPULATIVES
"Stack" or "Build"
"Put together"
"Triangle" (or other shape)
"Six" (or other number card)

LINING UP
"Coat"
"Open door"
"Me first"
"Go"

READING
"Turn the page"
Name of book
"Read"
"Who's that?"

COMMUNITY WALK
"Go to store"
"Look!"
"My shoe's untied" (request for help)
Reaching hand towards yours

ART ACTIVITIES
Reaching for crayons
"I need a brush"
"Glue"
"Hang it up"

Encouraging Social Interactions and Conversations

EXAMPLES OF LEADING STATEMENTS

Below are samples for providing opportunities for students to ask "wh" questions. It is important to note that this is not a script, but shows potential responses the student could make. Your goal is to encourage natural conversation, so it is not considered incorrect if a student responds with a different type of question than you expected unless it doesn't make sense in context.

PROMPTING WHAT QUESTIONS

TEACHER STATEMENT	POTENTIAL STUDENT RESPONSE
"You'll never believe what I saw this morning!"	"What did you see?"
"I had so much fun this weekend."	"What did you do?"
"I saw a terrible movie last night."	"What movie did you see?"
"Look at this bruise."	"What happened?"
"I played with a really silly toy today."	"What was the toy?"

PROMPTING WHO QUESTIONS

TEACHER STATEMENT	POTENTIAL STUDENT RESPONSE
"Guess who I saw yesterday!"	"Who did you see?"
"Look at the gift I just got."	"Who gave it to you?"
"Do you know who wrote this book?"	"No. Who wrote it?"
"We're receiving a visit today."	"Who is visiting?"
"I drove here with two people."	"Who did you drive with?"

PROMPTING WHERE QUESTIONS

TEACHER STATEMENT	POTENTIAL STUDENT RESPONSE
"I put your book in a special spot."	"Where did you put it?"
"Did you see the picture she drew?"	"No. Where is it?"
"I left my hat somewhere."	"Where did you leave it?"
"We're meeting them for dinner."	"Where are we meeting them?"
"I found the answer."	"Where did you find it?"

Encouraging Social Interactions and Conversations

PROMPTING WHEN QUESTIONS	
TEACHER STATEMENT	POTENTIAL STUDENT RESPONSE
"I saw that movie, too."	"When did you see it?"
"We are going to the store today."	"When are we going?"
"You wouldn't believe what time I woke up."	"When did you wake up?"
"I've had this shirt for a long time."	"When did you get it?"
"We can't look at the book yet."	"When can we look at it?"

PROMPTING WHY QUESTIONS	
TEACHER STATEMENT	POTENTIAL STUDENT RESPONSE
"I had to move the car."	"Why did you have to move the car?"
"We are having snack time earlier today."	"Why is snack time earlier?"
"My foot is still hurting."	"Why is it hurting?"
"We can't use the computer today."	"Why not?"
"The playground is closed."	"Why is it closed?"

APPENDIX

C

Data Sheets and Samples

Per Opportunity Individual Data Sheet

Teaching Procedure: The following should be explained in detail for each step: date implemented, pre-test score, number of trials per session, S^D, response definition, prompt level, error correction procedure, and mastery criterion.

Computation Procedure: Take the total number of correct responses and divide by the total number of opportunities and multiply by 100 for a percentage (# correct ÷ # of opportunities x 100 = %). Graph accordingly on the corresponding *Per Opportunity Graph*.

Per Opportunity Individual Data Sheet

STUDENT: *Stephanie*   STRAND/DOMAIN: *Geometry*

PROMPT LEVEL ABBREVIATIONS:

FPP – Full Physical Prompt
PPP – Partial Physical Prompt
M – Modeling
GP – Gestural Prompt
VP – Verbal Prompt
VSP – Visual Prompt

DATE	CCSS CODE	TARGET	PROMPT LEVELS AND RESPONSE RECORDING (Y/N)										PERCENT CORRECT	INSTRUCTOR INITIALS
2/11/15	1.G.A.2	Triangle	Ⓨ N	Y Ⓝ GP	Ⓨ N GP	Ⓨ N	Ⓨ N	Ⓨ N	Y Ⓝ	—	—	—	70%	TR
2/12/15	1.G.A.2	Triangle	Ⓨ N GP	Ⓨ N GP	Ⓨ N	Ⓨ N	Ⓨ N	Y Ⓝ GP	—	—	—	—	80%	TR
			Y/N	Y/N	Y/N	Y/N	Y/N	Y/N	Y/N	Y/N	Y/N	Y/N		
			Y/N	Y/N	Y/N	Y/N	Y/N	Y/N	Y/N	Y/N	Y/N	Y/N		
			Y/N	Y/N	Y/N	Y/N	Y/N	Y/N	Y/N	Y/N	Y/N	Y/N		
			Y/N	Y/N	Y/N	Y/N	Y/N	Y/N	Y/N	Y/N	Y/N	Y/N		
			Y/N	Y/N	Y/N	Y/N	Y/N	Y/N	Y/N	Y/N	Y/N	Y/N		
			Y/N	Y/N	Y/N	Y/N	Y/N	Y/N	Y/N	Y/N	Y/N	Y/N		
			Y/N	Y/N	Y/N	Y/N	Y/N	Y/N	Y/N	Y/N	Y/N	Y/N		

Per Opportunity Individual Data Sheet

STUDENT: _____ STRAND/DOMAIN: _____

PROMPT LEVEL ABBREVIATIONS:

FPP — Full Physical Prompt   **M** — Modeling   **VP** — Verbal Prompt
PPP — Partial Physical Prompt   **GP** — Gestural Prompt   **VSP** — Visual Prompt

DATE	CCSS CODE	TARGET	PROMPT LEVELS AND RESPONSE RECORDING (Y/N)									PERCENT CORRECT	INSTRUCTOR INITIALS
			Y/N	Y/N	Y/N	Y/N	Y/N	Y/N	Y/N				
			Y/N	Y/N	Y/N	Y/N	Y/N	Y/N	Y/N				
			Y/N	Y/N	Y/N	Y/N	Y/N	Y/N	Y/N				
			Y/N	Y/N	Y/N	Y/N	Y/N	Y/N	Y/N				
			Y/N	Y/N	Y/N	Y/N	Y/N	Y/N	Y/N				
			Y/N	Y/N	Y/N	Y/N	Y/N	Y/N	Y/N				
			Y/N	Y/N	Y/N	Y/N	Y/N	Y/N	Y/N				
			Y/N	Y/N	Y/N	Y/N	Y/N	Y/N	Y/N				
			Y/N	Y/N	Y/N	Y/N	Y/N	Y/N	Y/N				

Per Opportunity Group Data Sheet

For this example, the teacher was doing a whole group geometry lesson using tiles from the *Shape Shuffle*. She had this data sheet on a clipboard so she could take data for all of the students during the activity. (It may also be beneficial to have a paraprofessional take data while you conduct the activity.) She mixed in mastered questions with the questions focused on the target skill, but only marked Yes or No for the questions focused on the target skill. She only circled Y for a student if the student independently responded correctly without any prompts. She was able to use the shape tiles to practice the target skills, rotating around the group and providing appropriate reinforcement for correct responses as well as for appropriate circle time behaviors.

Per Opportunity Group Data Sheet

PROGRAM: *Geometry*

CCSS: *1.G.A.2/1.G.A.3*

STUDENT	TARGET	RESPONSES	PERCENT CORRECT
Carlos	labels "half" of a circle	Y/N circles	60%
Mark	combines two squares to make a rectangle	Y/N circles	40%
Lisa	combines two half circles to make a circle	Y/N circles	100%
James	labels "quarter of" for four equal parts of a rectangle	Y/N circles	50%
Diego	combines two half circles to make a circle	Y/N circles	30%
Daquan	combines two triangles to make a square	Y/N circles	80%

Different Roads to Learning | ABA Curriculum for the Common Core

Per Opportunity Group Data Sheet

PROGRAM: _____

CCSS: _____

STUDENT	TARGET	RESPONSES					PERCENT CORRECT
		Y / N	Y / N	Y / N	Y / N	Y / N	
		Y / N	Y / N	Y / N	Y / N	Y / N	
		Y / N	Y / N	Y / N	Y / N	Y / N	
		Y / N	Y / N	Y / N	Y / N	Y / N	
		Y / N	Y / N	Y / N	Y / N	Y / N	
		Y / N	Y / N	Y / N	Y / N	Y / N	
		Y / N	Y / N	Y / N	Y / N	Y / N	
		Y / N	Y / N	Y / N	Y / N	Y / N	
		Y / N	Y / N	Y / N	Y / N	Y / N	
		Y / N	Y / N	Y / N	Y / N	Y / N	
		Y / N	Y / N	Y / N	Y / N	Y / N	
		Y / N	Y / N	Y / N	Y / N	Y / N	

Per Opportunity Graph

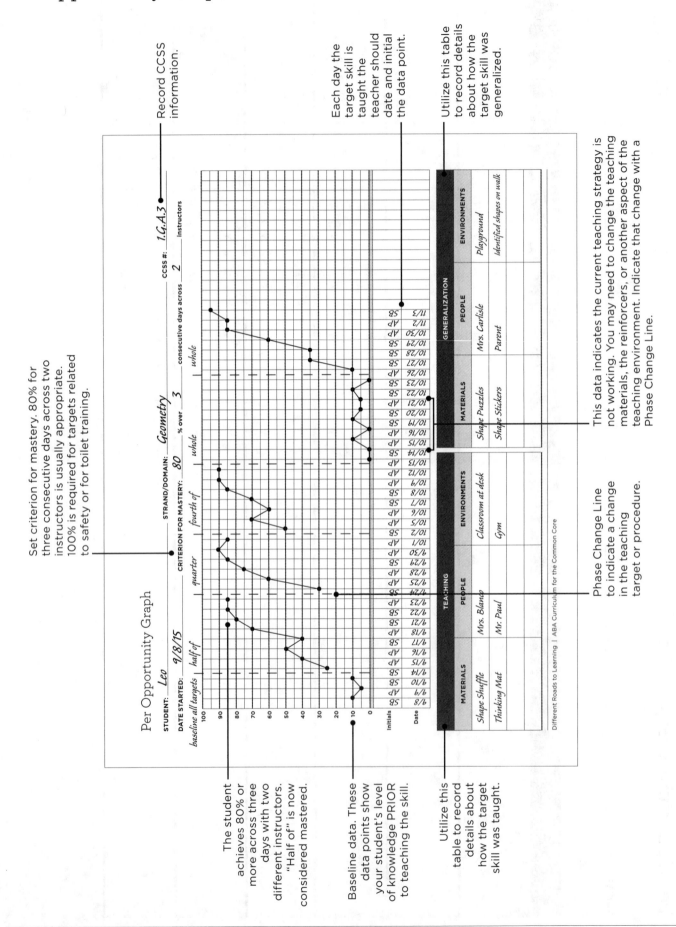

Record CCSS information.

Each day the target skill is taught the teacher should date and initial the data point.

Utilize this table to record details about how the target skill was generalized.

Set criterion for mastery. 80% for three consecutive days across two instructors is usually appropriate. 100% is required for targets related to safety or for toilet training.

The student achieves 80% or more across three days with two different instructors. "Half of" is now considered mastered.

Baseline data. These data points show your student's level of knowledge PRIOR to teaching the skill.

Utilize this table to record details about how the target skill was taught.

This data indicates the current teaching strategy is not working. You may need to change the teaching materials, the reinforcers, or another aspect of the teaching environment. Indicate that change with a Phase Change Line.

Phase Change Line to indicate a change in the teaching target or procedure.

Per Opportunity Graph

STUDENT: _____ STRAND/DOMAIN: _____ CCSS #: _____

DATE STARTED: _____ CRITERION FOR MASTERY: _____ % over _____ consecutive days across _____ instructors

	100																						
	90																						
	80																						
	70																						
	60																						
	50																						
	40																						
	30																						
	20																						
	10																						
	0																						
Initials																							
Date																							

TEACHING			GENERALIZATION		
MATERIALS	PEOPLE	ENVIRONMENTS	MATERIALS	PEOPLE	ENVIRONMENTS

Task Analysis: *Total Task*

Below is a sample of a task analysis created for the skill of washing hands. The student earns a + for independently completing the step. If any type of prompt is required, the prompt level is recorded next to the step. At the bottom, the percentage correct is determined by dividing the number of independently performed steps by the total number of steps.

A task analysis can be completed in one of three ways. The first is a whole task analysis, in which the student is taught the entire chain of tasks at the same time.

The second is forward chaining, in which the student is taught the first step in the chain, while all other steps are done for them. Once that step is mastered, the student is then taught the next step and expected to do the first and second step independently. This continues until all steps are learned.

The final way to teach a task analysis is through backwards chaining. This is similar to forward chaining, except the adult does all the steps for the child, and the child completes the last step. Once the student has mastered that step, then they are taught the next-to-last step and expected to do that and the last step independently. This continues until all steps are learned.

Task Analysis: *Total Task*

STUDENT: *Brian*   TASK: *Washing hands*   DATE PROGRAM STARTED: *02/01/15*

PROMPT LEVEL ABBREVIATIONS:

FPP — Full Physical Prompt   M — Modeling   VP — Verbal Prompt
PPP — Partial Physical Prompt   GP — Gestural Prompt   VSP — Visual Prompt

DATE	02/01	02/02	02/03	02/04	02/05	02/08	02/09	02/10					
STEP #	COMPONENT SKILL				PROMPT LEVELS								
1	Push up sleeves (if necessary)	FPP	PPP	PPP	GP	+	+	+	+				
2	Turn on water	FPP	FPP	PPP	PPP	PPP	VP	VP	VP				
3	Wet hands	PPP	+	+	+	+	+	+	+				
4	Push pump to put soap in hand	FPP	FPP	PPP	PPP	+	+	+	+				
5	Scrub hands for 10 seconds	FPP	PPP	PPP	GP	GP	+	+	+				
6	Rinse hands	FPP	GP	+	+	+	+	+	+				
7	Turn off water	FPP	GP	+	+	+	+	+	+				
8	Dry hands on towel	FPP	FPP	PPP	PPP	PPP	GP	GP	GP				
	PERCENT CORRECT	0%	12.5%	37.5%	37.5%	62.5%	75%	75%	75%				

Task Analysis: *Forward Chaining*

For this example, the teacher starts by teaching the student to independently push up his sleeves. Once he has done that independently two times in a row, the teacher introduces the next step.

Task Analysis: *Forward Chaining*

STUDENT: *Brian*   TASK: *Washing hands*   DATE PROGRAM STARTED: *02/01/15*

PROMPT LEVEL ABBREVIATIONS:

FPP — Full Physical Prompt
PPP — Partial Physical Prompt
M — Modeling
GP — Gestural Prompt
VP — Verbal Prompt
VSP — Visual Prompt

STEP #	COMPONENT SKILL	02/01	02/02	02/03	02/04	02/05	02/08	02/09	02/10
	DATE					PROMPT LEVELS			
1	Push up sleeves (if necessary)	PPP	PPP	GP	+	+	+	+	+
2	Turn on water					GP	GP	+	+
3	Wet hands								GP
4	Push pump to put soap in hand								
5	Scrub hands for 10 seconds								
6	Rinse hands								
7	Turn off water								
8	Dry hands on towel								
	PERCENT CORRECT	0%	0%	0%	12.5%	12.5%	12.5%	25%	25%

Task Analysis: *Backward Chaining*

For this example, the teacher starts by teaching the student to independently dry his hands after the teacher has taken him through all the other steps. Once he has done that independently two times in a row, the teacher introduces the previous step.

Task Analysis: _Backward Chaining_

STUDENT: _Brian_   **TASK:** _Washing hands_   **DATE PROGRAM STARTED:** _02/01/15_

PROMPT LEVEL ABBREVIATIONS:

FPP — Full Physical Prompt
PPP — Partial Physical Prompt
M — Modeling
GP — Gestural Prompt
VP — Verbal Prompt
VSP — Visual Prompt

STEP #	COMPONENT SKILL	02/01	02/02	02/03	02/04	02/05	02/08	02/09	02/10
					PROMPT LEVELS				
1	Push up sleeves (if necessary)								
2	Turn on water								
3	Wet hands								
4	Push pump to put soap in hand								
5	Scrub hands for 10 seconds								
6	Rinse hands						PPP	PPP	PPP
7	Turn off water				GP	+	+	+	+
8	Dry hands on towel	PPP	GP	+	+	+	+	+	+
	PERCENT CORRECT	0%	0%	12.5%	12.5%	25%	25%	25%	25%

Different Roads to Learning | ABA Curriculum for the Common Core

Task Analysis: _____

STUDENT: _____ TASK: _____ DATE PROGRAM STARTED: _____

PROMPT LEVEL ABBREVIATIONS:

FPP — Full Physical Prompt M — Modeling VP — Verbal Prompt
PPP — Partial Physical Prompt GP — Gestural Prompt VSP — Visual Prompt

DATE															
STEP #	COMPONENT SKILL					PROMPT LEVELS									
PERCENT CORRECT															

References

Application to students with disabilities. (2014).
Retrieved from http://corestandards.org/assets/application-to-students-with-disabilities.pdf

Cooper, J.O., Heron, T.E., & Heward, W.L. (2007). Applied behavior analysis (2nd ed.).
Upper Saddle River, NJ: Pearson Prentice Hall.

Fovel, J.T. (2013). The new ABA program companion. M.F. Danielski (Ed.). New York, NY: DRL Books.

Larsson, E.V., & Wright, S. (2011). I. Ovar Lovaas (1927–2010). *The Behavior Analyst, 34*(1): 111–114.

Leaf, R., & McEachin, J. (Eds.). (1999). A work in progress. New York, NY: DRL Books.

Lovaas, O.I. (1987). Behavioral treatment and normal educational and intellectual functioning
in young autistic children. *Journal of Consulting and Clinical Psychology*, 55, 3-9.

McClannahan, L.E., & Kranz, P.J. (2005). Teaching conversation to children with autism:
Scripts and script fading. Bethesda, MD: Woodbine House.

McEachin, J.J., Smith, T., & Lovaas, O.I. (1993). Long-term outcome for children with autism who received
early intensive behavioral treatment. *American Journal on Mental Retardation*, 97(4): 359-372.

Rispoli, M., O'Reilly, M., Lang, R., Machalicek, W., Davis, T., Lancioni, Giulio, & Sigafoos, J. (2011).
Effects of Motivating Operations on Problem and Academic Behavior in Classrooms.
Journal of Applied Behavior Analysis, 44, 187-192.

Sundberg, M.L., & Partington, J.W. (1999). The need for both discrete trial and natural environment
language training for children with autism. In P.M. Ghezzi, W.L. Williams, & J.E. Carr (Eds.),
Autism: Behavior-analytic perspectives (pp. 139-156). Reno, NJ: Context Press.

Taylor, B.A., & Harris, S.L. (1995). Teaching children with autism to seek information:
Acquisition of novel information and generalization of responding.
Journal of Applied Behavior Analysis, 28, 3-14.

Weiss, M.J., & Valbona, D. (2011). Jumpstarting communication skills in children with autism.
Bethesda, MD: Woodbine House.